The
Marriage of Anansewa
a storytelling drama

Efua T. Sutherland

Longman

Longman Group Limited London

Associated companies, branches and
representatives throughout the world

First published 1975

ISBN 0 582 64139 X

Printed in Great Britain by
Western Printing Services Ltd, Bristol

Foreword

There is in Ghana a story-telling art called *Anansesɛm* by Akan-speaking people. The name, which literally means Ananse stories, is used both for the body of stories told and for the story-telling performance itself. Although this story-telling is usually a domestic activity, there are in existence some specialist groups who have given it a full theatrical expression with established conventions. It is this system of traditional theatre which I have developed and classified as *Anansegoro*. A consideration of some of the conventions of Anansesɛm will reveal the bases of *The Marriage of Anansewa*.

Who is Ananse, and why should so many stories be told about him? Ananse appears to represent a kind of Everyman, artistically exaggerated and distorted to serve society as a medium for self-examination. He has a penetrating awareness of the nature and psychology of human beings and animals. He is also made to mirror in his behaviour fundamental human passions, ambitions and follies as revealed in contemporary situations. Significantly, laughter is the main social response to Ananse as a character. In addition, it is in the verbal comments which often underscore the laughter that society's attitude to him is clarified. Of these the most representative is 'Ananse's wealth!'—a sarcastic expression for successes and triumphs which are not likely to last. Indeed most of Ananse's successes are doubtful and temporary. By constantly over-reaching himself he ruins his schemes and ends up impoverished. That Ananse is, artistically, a medium for society to criticise itself can be seen in the expression, 'Exterminate Ananse, and society will be ruined.'

The stories are composed with performance demands in mind and in a number of different forms and styles. Most are in a combination of narrative prose and a poetry which is meant to be sung or rhythmically recited on the basis of solo and choral response.

However, the stories are not rigidly formed. Every one is intended to be given fuller composition and artistic interpretation by the Storyteller. He tries to prove his artistry by refreshing and up-dating his story by spontaneous improvisation as he tells it. And it is to this artistry in the narration that the audience look for the aesthetic experience they seek. Thus, stories in the tradition are under constant revision for renewal and development. Also, contemporary interest inspires the composition of completely new stories to replenish the repertoire.

The Storyteller in Anansesɛm tells the whole story himself. *The Marriage of Anansewa* demonstrates how this role has been adapted in Anansegoro. Here the narrator is still seen as the owner of the story with a conventional right to know everything, to have a right to be personally involved in the action and to be capable of inducing his audience to believe they are there with him and similarly involved. Likewise, the convention of the Storyteller having a staff in imitation of an Okyeame, a Chief's official spokesman, is adapted.

In Anansesɛm musical performances are called *Mboguo*. Many of the Mboguo are part and parcel of the stories themselves and are performed in context, led by the Storyteller. But it is a convention for Mboguo to be contributed by other people present. They are permitted to halt the narration of a story to make such contributions, and always their choices are prompted by some sort of inspiration in the performance situation. Contributed Mboguo may be reflective of a mood or aimed at quickening the pace of the performance or inspiring the general assembly. It is not uncommon for some contributions to be made merely from a high-spirited desire to show off! Anybody may dance when the musical interlude is open to general participation. Interludes of mimed action and comic playlets are also contributed, but strictly by specialist performers who do the acting while sharing the performance of the accompanying music with the rest of the assembly.

A typical story-telling session opens with a series of rousing Mboguo songs led by a specialist group's signature tune. Some groups even include in this introduction the performance of a semi-serious, semi-playful Mboguo of libation. Directly afterwards the Storyteller begins to perform and from then on the programme is organised on a system of serialising the story by breaking up the narration at various points with different kinds of Mboguo. The session ends with the specialist group's signing-off Mboguo song.

The singing of Mboguo songs is usually accompanied by hand-clapping with slightly cupped hands and drumming, with castanets and a gong instrument providing the rhythmic control.

Mboguo in its traditional concept and usage has been inherited wholesale by Anansegoro. However, in addition it can be used to develop action and characterisation, or to acquaint the audience with shifts of time or place.

Anansesɛm is a community art. All the people present are performers in one way or another, either actively or potentially. Though the specialists control the main flow of the action, their performance requires the participation of the audience.

People come to a session prepared to be, in story-telling parlance, 'hoaxed'. The term is used in its humorous sense, and meant to be a joke in itself. Hence in the course of a particularly entrancing story it is normal for an appreciative listener to engage in the following exchange:

LISTENER: Keep hoaxing me! (*Sisi me!*)
NARRATOR: I am hoaxing you and will keep on hoaxing you!
 (*Mirisisi wo, mesisi wo bio!*)

The formula is practically a form of applause, an encouragement to the Storyteller to sustain his artistry.

Of the many problems I have encountered in composing Anansegoro, the most tricky has been how to invest it with some capacity for invoking this element of community participation. I have used the device of moving on to the stage a pool of *Players* representing both the specialist performers and the participating audience of Anansesɛm. The onus for making the public audience feel at one with the on-stage participating audience is of course on the director of the play.

Efua T. Sutherland

Acknowledgement

The publishers would like to thank Willis E. Bell for permission to publish the photographs.

Cast

PLAYERS

All performers in the play, grouped together as a unified pool of music-makers, dancers, actors, *and as a participating audience*. Provision must be made for able song-leaders, one or two drummers and, if possible, a guitarist. When necessary actors simply detach themselves from the pool at convenient times to dress, returning when their roles are over

PROPERTY MAN

Serves primarily as property manager, manning a property stand on-stage, and distributing props on cue. In addition, he does scene-setting duties, and is conveniently available as an actor for supporting roles. He can function, if necessary, as a prompter, and quite openly, provided he does it with skilful informality. When *free*, he is responsive to the action of the pool of PLAYERS or of the actors on stage

ANANSE

ANANSEWA

Ananse's daughter

POST OFFICE CREW

Any effective number. Other PLAYERS are free to participate by doing make-believe business at the Post Office

STORYTELLER

AKWASI AND AKOSUA

A young couple

POSTMAN

SAPAASE MESSENGERS

Two women, matronly

CAST

CHIEF-WHO-IS-CHIEF'S MESSENGER	The image of a high-grade diplomat
AYA	Ananse's mother
EKUWA	Ananse's aunt
CHRISTIE	Miss Christina Yamoah, a fashionable woman
GIRLS	About six, of Anansewa's age-group
TWO WOMEN	For the dirge
MESSENGERS	To the 'funeral'
1 From the Mines	Two men
2 From Sapaase	One man and two women
3 From Akate	Two men
4 From Chief-Who-Is-Chief	The 'diplomat', another man and two or three women

The Marriage of Anansewa is published after productions of the play in Akan and in English by three different companies in Ghana: the Workers' Brigade Drama Group, Kusum Agoromba (Kusum Players) and the Drama Studio Players and Kusum Agoromba combined.

Act One

[*The* PLAYERS *enter from one side of the stage, which is a bare room except for a small table and chair, centre, and start the play with a popular song.*]

PLAYERS:

Oh life is a struggle,
Oh life is a pain;
Oh life is a struggle,
Oh life is a pain
In this world.

Life is a struggle,
Citizens,
Life is a pain
In this world.

Life is a struggle,
Friends,
Life is a pain
In this world.

[*Halfway through the song,* ANANSE *enters hastily, escaping from the rain outside. He is wearing a shabby raincoat. At the entrance, he receives an old umbrella from* PROPERTY MAN, *and as he opens it up shakes off the rain. He shakes his head like a troubled man. Then, taking over the solo parts of the song, he walks round with umbrella aloft, clearly indicating that the song he is singing recounts his own story to the* PLAYERS *and the audience.*]

ANANSE: [*When the song is over*] While life is whipping you, rain also pours down to whip you some more. Whatever it was that man did wrong at the beginning of things must have been really awful for all of us to have to suffer so. [*He calls:*]

Anansewa—a! Where is that typewriter of yours? Bring it here. [*Pause.*] I've been thinking, thinking and thinking, until my head is earthquaking. Won't somebody who thinks he has discovered the simple solution for living this life kindly step forward and help out the rest of us? [*To the audience:*] Brother, could it be you? Mother, how about you? Nobody?

> Oh the world is hard,
> Is hard,
> The world is really hard.

[*Taking off his raincoat and calling again*] Anansewa—a! Where is that typewriter I bought for you at a price that nearly drove me to sell myself? Bring it here. [*He closes up the umbrella.*]

[*Enter* ANANSEWA *dressed for going out, and receives the typewriter from* PROPERTY MAN.]

ANANSEWA: Oh father, is it raining?

ANANSE: Yes, it's raining. It's rain combining with life to beat your father down. [*He leans the umbrella against the wall.*]

ANANSEWA: Oh. I didn't even know you were not in the house.

ANANSE: Going-and-coming is necessary. [*He takes off the raincoat and hands it over to* PROPERTY MAN.] Otherwise nothing succeeds. I went to buy paper. Here is typing paper. Here is carbon paper. Here are envelopes. [*He takes these items one by one from* PROPERTY MAN *and piles them in* ANANSEWA's *arms.*] Sit down with the machine.

ANANSEWA: [*Petulantly*] Ah, I was coming to tell you I was going out.

ANANSE: My daughter, it isn't well with the home, therefore sit down, open up the machine I bought for your training, and let the tips of your fingers give some service from the training for which I'm paying. I have very urgent letters to write.

ANANSEWA: Just when I was going out?

ANANSE: Daughter mine, it's your future I'm thinking about, so put the machine down and get ready to help me.

> Take paper,
> Get set,

> While I reflect;
> Get set,
> While I collect
> My thoughts together.

[*Walking about.*] I am stirring up all the brains in my head.

> Take paper
> While I cogitate.

ANANSEWA: [*Frowning with disappointment*] I'm ready.

ANANSE: Don't frown, my daughter. Have patience with your father. You are a child yet, in spite of your body's development. You cannot see as far as your father can. There you sit looking lovely, and it's exciting for you to go out in all your beauty. That is all you know. But, tell me, won't you return home, here, afterwards?

ANANSEWA: I will return home, here; why not?

ANANSE: And when you return, will your fees for E.P.'s Secretarial School be paid?

ANANSEWA: No.

ANANSE: Haven't you stayed at home for nearly two weeks because your fees are owing? And am I not still straining to find the money?

ANANSEWA: Yes.

ANANSE: I point it out to you, that the principal of E.P.'s Secretarial School—miser that he is—will remain merciless; that he will not hear of your returning unless I pay; unless you are carrying the money in your hands. Right or wrong?

ANANSEWA: [*Getting more unhappy*] Right.

ANANSE: Ahaa! Now let's turn our attention to that object there. That machine. That typewriter. After you have gone out and returned home, here, will the last instalment on that typewriter which you need for your training be paid? Eh?

ANANSEWA: No.

ANANSE: Good. So you agree there is need.

ANANSEWA: Oh, I know it.

ANANSE: And on whom is the burden of that need?

ANANSEWA: On you, father.

ANANSE: Well said; correct. Then, in that case, let me turn your attention to me a little. Take a look at my condition. I'm not young, and yet what are my prospects? To what can I look forward? After you have gone out and returned home, here, will my hope for a more comfortable future be any better? The mattress on which I try to rest my bones after each day's up-and-down—will it have changed from a straw-stuffed, lumpy mattress to a soft, bouncy Dunlopillo?

ANANSEWA: No. Oh, father, please . . .

ANANSE: I haven't finished. Apart from things like that, and above all, when you return, will there be a better, leak-proof roof over our heads? Let alone some comfortable chairs to sit in? A 'fridge in the kitchen? A car in the garage? My name on invitation lists for state functions? Embassies' parties? Tell me, tell me. Will I be able to go to memorial services, this week in a fine cloth, next week in a suit or a different cloth? Will I be able, if I go, to thrust my hand confidently into my pocket in public and take out a five-guinea donation?

ANANSEWA: [*Miserably*] Father, you have said enough, please.

ANANSE: Let me add one or two things more. Imagine a great congregation at church on an important occasion. It is time for the collection. There sits the priest. There stands the gleaming collection plate in everybody's view.

They call out: 'Those born on Sunday.' Those born on Sunday, the Kwesis and Esis,* rise, walk up, and deposit their money in the plate. 'Those born on Monday'. The Kodwos and Adwowas file up; they deposit.

It is coming soon to those born on Wednesday, mark you. To the Kwekus and Ekuwas. And my name is Kweku. Tell me, how many times have I missed going to church because there is nothing in my pocket to deposit in full view of the public? And after you have gone out and returned home, here, will I be any better off for going to church?

ANANSEWA: I implore you, father, I'm ready.

ANANSE: Finally, when I breathe my last and die, will my coffin be drawn in a fine, private hearse instead of a municipal hearse?

* Kwesis and Esis, etc. For some people in Ghana, there are sets of feminine and masculine names related to the names of the seven days of the week. They are known as Day Names. and people born on a particular day have an automatic right to whichever Day Name is relevant to them.

Will the people who come to my funeral eat salad and small
chops and drink good whisky, instead of chewing bits of cola
and drinking cheap gin and diluted Fanta? Tell me.

ANANSEWA: Father, why? I thought you . . .

ANANSE: [*Sharply*] Begin the typing. 'Dear Chief of Sapa . . .'

ANANSEWA: [*Hesitating*] So, father, do you desire all those things?
Haven't you condemned many of them often and often? You
have pooh-poohed them, haven't you?

ANANSE: Of course I have. Some of them are absolutely absurd.
Empty vanities. But you see, my child, I'm trying to use this
index to show you how all is not well at home. So set your
machine talking to help your father out. [*Walking away*.] As a
result of a most severe cracking of my brains, I'm at last able to
see a little hope gleaming in our future, and I'm directing my
steps towards it.

ANANSEWA: [*Busy at the machine*] Yes?

ANANSE: [*Absent-mindedly*] Step by step, my feet are in motion
under the direction of my mind, and I'm on the road to free you
and me from want. I'm not saying I want that much. But what
if a few things can come my way . . . if a few things . . . a few
things can come. . . . I'm not saying I'll eat chicken every day,
but what about a little fish today, and tomorrow, a little meat
on which I can count? I'm not saying my only daughter Anansewa must become a Judge of the Supreme Court . . . but what
about her finishing her secretarial course? And perhaps . . . well
. . . perhaps . . .

ANANSEWA: [*Having tried several times to get his attention by tapping on
the typewriter keys:*] He's forgotten I'm here. This absent-
mindedness of father's is most trying. [*Louder*] Oh, father,
please hurry.

ANANSE: What's that?

ANANSEWA: [*Louder still*] Rea—dy! The ty—ping!

ANANSE: [*Crisply*] Address;
today's date;
and cancel that 'Dear Chief of Sapa', it is too ordinary.

ANANSEWA: [*Typing*] Yes?

ANANSE: Cancel that, and put what I'm going to recite in its
place.
[*He assumes the stance of an official praise-singer.*]

'O Mighty-Tree-Of-Ancient-Origin!
Mighty-Tree-Of-Ancient-Origin,
Rooted in the shrine of deity!
Countless branches in which
Benighted wandering birds
Are welcome to shelter.'

ANANSEWA: All of that? All that in the place where 'Dear Chief of Sapa' should go? Is this a letter? How can I fit it in?
ANANSE: Fit it in. Chiefs adore their appellations.

[ANANSEWA *types vigorously for a while. At a signal from her,* ANANSE *continues his dictation.*]

'I have returned safely home after my visit to you. The little affair about which we spoke seriously occupies my thoughts. How can I ever forget that you have done me great honour? To show my gratitude, I will guard the object of your interest . . . with all the vigilance in my power.

'Now, I know that you who are seated on the ancient stools of our land know the a.b.c. of all our cherished laws, all our time-honoured customs.

'Since forwardness has never been one of my faults, I will not even dare to drop a hint that the way is open for you now to begin oiling the wheels of custom. You who do not pay mere lip service to law and custom but really live by them, need no prompting from anyone.

'Therefore I will only add that I'm very happy to be,

'Yours in the closest of links in the not too distant future,

'George Kweku Ananse.'

ANANSEWA: [*Enjoying her own performance*] Got it. Ah, father, your lips are sugared.
ANANSE: The address is Chief Sapa, The Palace, Sapaase.
ANANSEWA: Next?
ANANSE: The same letter is going to two other Chiefs. All you need is their appellations. Take them down in shorthand and as you work, I'll turn the last letter over in my mind.
ANANSEWA: I'm listening.
ANANSE: Here's one. [*He assumes the proper stance.*]

> 'Prickly-Pear!
> Cactus keeping guard
> On your territory's border,
> To your left your territory,
> To your right the sea;
> Tough and vigilant one,
> Thanks to your prickles
> The enemy bleeds,
> Thanks to your capacious leaves,
> Those whom you love
> Will always find within them
> Water to refresh them.'

ANANSEWA: Very nice.
ANANSE: Address: Togbe Klu IV, Akate.
ANANSEWA: Next?
ANANSE: [*With relish and vigour*]

> 'You are coming again,
> Aren't you?
> You are coming again?
>
> Oh, where shall we sit?
> Where shall we sit,
> When driver ants
> Are astir
> All over our ground?'

ANANSEWA: And whose appellation is that?
ANANSE: [*Secretively*] He whose appellation it is, has command of priceless lands. He is not small at all, Chief of . . . (*He whispers conspiratorially into Anansewa's ear. She nods in understanding.*]

ANANSEWA: You said there was one more?
ANANSE: Indeed. Please type this one with utmost care. [*He recites with tremendous vigour and at great speed.*]

> Oh! Fire-Extinguisher!
> Fire-Extinguisher,
> You have caused flame flashes to darken,
> You have caused 'I'm Irreversible'
> To come to a full stop.

Blazing-Column-Of-Fire-Who-Says-I-
Will-Not-Be-Halted
Has come to a full stop.

Masculine-One-Destined-To-Contend-
To-Victory!
You consume fire, *abraw*.*

This you did, this you did,
And therefore do nations say
Well done, and well done, *abraw*
Have they not heard your fame?
When they hear your fame
Do they not acclaim you in praise-names?

Fire-Extinguishing-Victor who deserves appellations!

[ANANSEWA *is so frustrated by the speed and passion of his performance that she has not been able to keep up with him.*]

Have you got it down?
ANANSEWA: How could I? I've never taken dictation at such super-
sonic speed before. Say it slowly, please.

[*Relaxing now and savouring his eloquence,* ANANSE *repeats the recital.*]

ANANSEWA: [*Finished, and looking at her watch*] And that's the end,
isn't it?
ANANSE: Nearly. The letter to this one is different, and it is brief:
    'The thing you sent me by your most respected messenger
has reached me; and it is so unexpected, so welcome, that
whether I'm dreaming or not is still an undecided question.
    'Briefly, thank you, Nana. All is well with . . . the object of
your interest. I look forward to the time when—it—will come
out of my custody into your hands.
    'Most humbly, and delightedly yours.
                                    'George Kweku Ananse.'
ANANSEWA: Finished?

* *abraw*: a title.

ANANSE: [*With a sigh of relief:*] Finished.

ANANSEWA: Address?

ANANSE: To Chief-Who-Is-Chief!

ANANSEWA: Chief-Who-Is-Chief. Town?

ANANSE: Town unnecessary. It will get there with just that. Now please be quick or we shall miss the mail.

MBOGUO (*Interlude*)

[*The posting of the letters.* PROPERTY MAN *sets the Post Office, with a counter and a pillar box. Two men from among the* PLAYERS *rise to man the Post Office in a busy way.*]

ANANSE: Please hurry,
                  For time is nobody's friend.
                  Hurry,
                  For time will not wait for you.

[ANANSEWA *seals each letter and passes it to her father who hurries to the Post Office, buys a stamp, sticks it on, gets it stamped officially, and slips it in the pillar box. The* PLAYERS *sing in accompaniment:*]

                  Hurry, hurry,
                  Hurry down there;
                  Hurry, hurry,
                  Hurry down there.

                  Time is nobody's friend,
                  Time is nobody's friend,
                  Time is nobody's friend.

                  So hurry, hurry,
                  Hurry down there.
                  Hurry, hurry,
                  Hurry down there.

                  Time will not wait for you,
                  Time will not wait for you,
                  Time will not wait for you.

So hurry, hurry,
Hurry down there,
Hurry, hurry,
Hurry down there.

[ANANSE *has finished. He returns home.* ANANSEWA *brings him a chair.* PROPERTY MAN *moves out the Post Office props.*]

ANANSE: [*Falling into the chair*] I'm exhausted.

ANANSEWA: Yes, I'm tired myself.

ANANSE: You have done well. And now, if you will come closer, I have something to give you.

ANANSEWA: Really?

[*She moves closer.* ANANSE *takes a bulging wallet out of his pocket and counts out money, to her amazement.*]

ANANSE: Ten cedis, ten cedis, one hundred clean cedis. Altogether, one hundred and twenty cedis. Take that to the miserly principal of E.P.'s Secretarial School.

ANANSEWA: My fees?

ANANSE: Correct. You can return to school.

ANANSEWA: [*She drops to her knees, embraces her father and nestles her head on his chest.*] Oh, father.

ANANSE: [*With pleasure*] And now we shall see. My daughter, now we shall see which one of those four chiefs will make the best husband for you.

ANANSEWA: [*In consternation*] What!

ANANSE: [*Very tickled*] That's the story.

ANANSEWA: You sit there smilingly saying 'That's the story.' What's the story?

ANANSE: The letters you've just typed for me to post. That's the story.

ANANSEWA: What?

ANANSE: Of course.

ANANSEWA: Of course what? You're making me feel like crying. What have you done to me, eh? Eh? Who said I wanted to marry a chief, eh? Who told those old chiefs of yours? Have they ever seen me?

ANANSE: Who told you they are old? You've never set eyes on them. They, of course, have seen you.

ANANSEWA: Where?

ANANSE: They have seen your photographs.

ANANSEWA: [*Recalling*] Ah-h, that's why! That's why you went to so much trouble to get my photograph taken. You made such a fuss. 'Take one of her, full height. Sit down this time, Anansewa, and turn your face slightly to the right.' Oh father, there's cunning in your head. You are to be feared.

ANANSE: [*Flattered*] I'm glad you don't underestimate me.

ANANSEWA: I have found you out. The week after those photographs were taken—that was when you travelled. I've found you out; you went on tour to see your chiefs.

ANANSE: Certainly. I covered miles. I travelled the country, by bus, by train, by ferry-boat. I lobbied for introductions into palace after palace. I listened with ears alert. I observed with keen eyes. I assessed everything before I selected the four chiefs to whom I could show your photographs with advantage.

ANANSEWA: But why on earth four?

ANANSE: Oh, let's say that covers North, South, East and West.

ANANSEWA: How exasperating! Oh, my father is selling me, he is selling me. [*She clasps her neck and sings, the* PLAYERS *joining in.*]

> My father is selling me,
> Alas, alas!
> Whoever thought he would?
> Alas, alas!
>
> But let me tell you bluntly,
> I'll never comply.
> I will not let you sell me
> Like some parcel to a customer.
> > Not ever!
> > Not ever!
> > Not ever!
> > Not ever!

ANANSE: My daughter is a child.

ANANSEWA: I will not let you sell me like some parcel to a customer. [*She sings on.*]

> I will select my lover myself;
> I'll never comply.
> I will not let you sell me
> Like some parcel to a customer.
> > Not ever!
> > Not ever!

ANANSE: She is a child.

ANANSEWA: And do you really mean you're trying to tell me that those four chiefs of yours are satisfied with just photographs?

ANANSE: Oh, the photographs have slain them, have slain them flat. Your engagement is not far off at all.

ANANSEWA: I will not take part in any photograph engagement.

ANANSE: This daughter of mine doesn't know much about this world's ways.

ANANSEWA: What's this you've done to me? I'm not a child. I'm twenty.

ANANSE: She's not a child.
                She's twenty.
                And she still eats out of my pocket!
                Nonsense!

ANANSEWA: I'll stop eating.

ANANSE: I'll thank you if you stop. Say also, that you'll pay your own fees to the miserly principal of E.P.'s Secretarial School.

ANANSEWA: I'll stop attending then, and . . . Oh, you are making me miserable.

ANANSE: Talk on; you'll stop attending what and do what instead? Give me back the fees in your hand and stop attending, you fool, when in two months' time you could have your certificate in your hand?

ANANSEWA: Did I say I would stop attending anywhere? Did I? But bluntly speaking, as for some old chief with fifty wives, that won't do at all. Never. [*She is close to tears with her hands covering her face.*]

ANANSE: [*With cunning*] Supposing it isn't some old chief as you ignorantly describe, but the finely built, glowing black, large-eyed, handsome as anything, courageous and famous Chief-Who-Is-Chief?

ANANSEWA: [*Interested in such news*] Chief-Who-Is-Chief?

ANANSE: I mean, himself.

ANANSEWA: But who are we to have expectations about him?

ANANSE: You may well ask who are we. But just the same, you have just typed a letter which I have posted to him.

ANANSEWA: [*Amazed, and then with excitement*] I just typed it, of course. I, Anansewa, have typed a letter to Chief-Who-Is-Chief.

ANANSE: [*Proudly*] You think I'm walking round this world playing ludo?

ANANSEWA: [*Searching for the copy*] Is it I? Here is the letter. [*She reads . . .*] 'the object of your interest'. Is that me, father? Am I the object? Oh, I wish, I wish . . .

ANANSE: [*Pompously*] I will quote you what the rhesus monkey says. Rhesus monkey, it is he who says that unless he sees with his own eyes, he will not believe. He says, 'My eyes are my oracle.' Therefore, my child, if you want proof that Chief-Who-Is-Chief is interested in you, spread out your hand and look at what you are holding there.

ANANSEWA: [*She spreads out her hand and is amazed.*] It's my fees I've got in my hand.

ANANSE: How did I get that money, when for more than a month I have been constantly struggling with our poverty? I ask you. [ANANSEWA *is dumbfounded.*] Read the beginning of that letter.

ANANSEWA: [*Reading:*] 'The thing you sent by your most respected messenger has reached me . . .'

ANANSE: Stop just there. You are holding in your hand almost all of the full amount of that 'thing'. That 'thing' is the first solid proof that Chief-Who-Is-Chief is not just showing interest with his mouth. He is willing and eager to oil the wheels of custom; and therefore he has sent something for the maintenance of the object of his interest.

ANANSEWA: If this is the case, what do I do now? [*She sits down to think.*]

ANANSE: Stop eating, and stop attending school, as you said.

ANANSEWA: Oh, no, father. Have a little patience, for I'm thinking about it.

ANANSE: [*Deliberately piling it on*] All the toiling I have taken it upon myself to suffer for you. And you rise against me yelling, 'I will not let you sell me like some parcel to a customer'. O.K.

13

I won't sell you, so stop attending school, and cut short your training, and do without your certificate.

ANANSEWA: Please, be patient. What? Chief-Who-Is-Chief and I?

ANANSE: [Full of smiles] You think I'm walking around this world playing games?

ANANSEWA: [Embracing him] Oh, my loving father.

ANANSE: Oh, my lovely daughter. My foolish baby.

ANANSEWA: I wish, I wish . . .

ANANSE: So do I, so do I.

ANANSEWA: [Infatuated] Ah.

ANANSE: You have to say ah.

ANANSEWA: Ah. Mmm.

ANANSE: Does he appeal to you? That's how it is, isn't it? Tell the truth.

ANANSEWA: I'm amazed. Father, you are a wonder.

ANANSE: You see? As I'm standing here in my *colo** trousers, I'm not a man to be sneered at. I circulate. I'm capable of going and coming.

ANANSEWA: Feel my heart. It's thumping so fast.

ANANSE: Let it thump; don't prevent it.

ANANSEWA: What news is this that is so sweet? [She panics suddenly.] But . . . oh, father, what's this you have done?

ANANSE: Again? Have I done something else?

ANANSEWA: The other letters. The other three.

ANANSE: [Pretending unconcern] Yes?

ANANSEWA: The other chiefs. The other three.

ANANSE: Yes. So what about them?

ANANSEWA: [Picking up copies of the letters she has arranged beside the typewriter] Chief of Sapaase; Chief of Akate; and this other chief whose name is whispered in the ear. Four chiefs. But don't you see there's only one of me? [She is almost in tears.] What's this you've done to me?

ANANSE: [Who has been smiling all this while] Listen, my one and only daughter, what I have done is that I have organised around you a most lively competition.

ANANSEWA: But aren't you afraid?

ANANSE: [Nasally] Who said I wasn't afraid?

ANANSEWA: Then why are you doing it?

* *colo*: colonial; out of date; not in fashion.

ANANSE: I'm counting on human nature to help disentangle it. All four chiefs can't be winners, don't you see? Child, your father is trying for you. Don't ask too many complicated questions. Your father can only cope with one step at a time.

ANANSEWA: It's a very tangled affair.

ANANSE: So it is. I don't deny it. But, believe me, my child, if it looks as if I have tied a knot, I haven't tied it so tight that it cannot be untied. A little more thinking is all that is needed to untie this knot. Have confidence in your father. Return to school, tomorrow, pay your fees, and just concentrate on getting your certificate. [*Affectionately*] Do say something to comfort me. I'm tired. I need some rest.

ANANSEWA: [*Smiling with sympathy*] All right, father. I suppose I'll leave it all in your hands and trust you.

ANANSE: Many thanks.

ANANSEWA: [*Having checked on the rain outside*] It isn't raining too hard now.

ANANSE: It has quietened down, has it? Well, I don't feel quite so whipped by life as I did when I came in. If you still want to go out, why don't you?

ANANSEWA: I will, I think. [*She returns her typewriter to* PROPERTY MAN.] Have a good rest, father.

ANANSE: [*Accompanying her out*] Thank you, one and only. All shall be well.

[PROPERTY MAN *clears the stage*. STORYTELLER *rises from among the* PLAYERS *and receiving his staff from* PROPERTY MAN, *speaks to them.*]

STORYTELLER: Ananse certainly needs a rest after spinning such a web. [PLAYERS *roar with laughter*.] I was present when all this happened. [*To gong-player:*] Calling!

[*Gong rhythm starts up.*] Hands! [PLAYERS *start the clapping rhythm and* STORYTELLER *starts the song for the next MBOGUO, and sings it with the* PLAYERS.]

> She says, mmm mother;
> She says, mmm father;

> She says, how shall I find a mate?
> K-legged Ama,
>
> How shall I find a mate?
>
> Limping Ama,
>
> How shall I find a mate?

[*Two women from among the* PLAYERS *mime in a playful dance the deformity the song describes. When it ends one of the* SONG-LEADERS *interrupts the* STORYTELLER.]

SONGLEADER: Storyteller, hold your story for a while.
STORYTELLER: It's held for you, brother.

[SONGLEADER *starts off the chant* 'Kweku Ananse Said He Would'.]

> Kweku Ananse said he would!
> And he has done it
> He has done it
> O, mankind!

STORYTELLER: And that chant having passed away let me admit that I can feel a little for Ananse. I am a father myself. To tell you the truth, I wish I had a little bit of his kind of cunning.

It's very clear that he knows the customs more than well. Notice how he has them at his finger tips, spinning them out, weaving them into a design to suit his purposes.

It would be amazing if there was any among those four chiefs who didn't know that a man who desires to marry somebody's daughter *can* improve his chances by paying his way with gifts. Ananse has selected men who will do exactly as he hopes and do it properly too.

Oh, Ananse. His ways are certainly complicated. It's very possible that these chiefs will be drawn right into his net; and for this affair to turn into sheer profit for him. If negotiations have only reached this stage, is there any law binding him to give his daughter in marriage to any of those four chiefs?

PLAYERS: There is no such law.

[*Once more he starts off the song 'How shall I find a Mate?' and moves in dance to stand aside.*]

MBOGUO

AKWAWI AND AKOSUA

[AKOSUA *strides saucily in, crosses, and halts with arms akimbo among the* PLAYERS. AKWASI *enters in hot pursuit. He looks this way and that, not noticing where she is.*]

AKWASI: [*To* STORYTELLER:] Please sir, did a girl pass by, this
    way?
STORYTELLER: Do you mean that one standing over there?
AKWASI: Aha! Thank you, sir. Hey, Akosua, there you are, aren't
    you? [*He seizes her at the waist by her cloth* and pulls her out from the group.*]
AKOSUA: [*Stridently*] Let me go!
                Let me go!

AKWASI: I will not let you go.
                   I will not let you go.
                   You cannot spend my dough
                      And treat me so.
AKOSUA: You funny man,
                   Don't you know
                   I'm not your wife?
                   Am I your wife?
AKWASI: Don't you know you are?
AKOSUA: What law says that?
                   Quote me the law
                   That makes me your wife.

                   Oh, you'll make me laugh enough
                   To drive you to distraction.
                   How, how, and how
                   Do you come by such an assumption?

* cloth: dress.

17

AKWASI: I've brought you gifts,
I've bought you clothes
And shining jingling things
For your neck and for your wrists.

AKOSUA: So this is your character. You keep coming to me. 'Akosua, this is something small I bought for you', you say. I'm reluctant to accept it, but you press it on me. 'You'll embarrass me if you refuse it', so you say. Therefore, I accept it. And here you stand today in a public street screaming out that:

          I spend your dough
          And treat you so.
I have filed you in my mind for future reference.

AKWASI: I'm bawling you out like this because you're so persistently saucy.

AKOSUA: I'm not your wife,
So let me go!
AKWASI: Ask your mother,
Ask your father;
If you don't know
They do!
AKOSUA: Ha haa-a!
Oil is dripping into fire.

Akwasi, listen, come home with me then, and tell my parents I'm your wife, and see if they don't give you a slap that will spark fire in your eyes.

AKWASI: Do you suppose they're as senseless as you are?

AKOSUA: Oh, no, I don't think that at all. Quite the contrary, they are far wiser. They know I'm not your wife until after you have come to their home and placed the customary head-drink* on their table. [*Teasingly*] You see what I mean?

AKWASI: [*Disarmed*] So that's what you are saying.

AKOSUA: And about time too, don't you think? [*He lets her go.*] Ah, now you're letting me go. That's better. I've gained my per-

* head-drink: an important token by which the marriage is legally established; symbolised by a token sum of money and some drinks, and handed over formally on behalf of the prospective husband to members of the family of the prospective wife.

sonal freedom. Bye! Any time you're ready, bring my head-drink home to my parents.

And after that, I will stop when you call. I'll take care of your house. I'll sweep, I'll scrub, I'll wash your clothes, and I'll quarrel sweetly with you to your extreme delight. Bye! [*She laughs and skips teasingly off.*]

AKWASI: Ah! This girl is killing me. [*He turns back in miserable anger.*]

STORYTELLER: I say, young man! Gentleman! [AKWASI *stops.*] If you know that this girl is in the wrong, why don't you take her to court? [AKWASI *is hesitant.*] Sir, have you, by any chance, performed her head-drink ceremony?

AKWASI: Look, dad, whoever you are, don't make me wild. [*He stalks out, driven away by jeering laughter from the* PLAYERS.]

STORYTELLER: There you are. As I was saying, it is possible for Ananse to profit from the gifts his daughter's suitors bring, and not be bound by any obligation at all.

What craftiness. Also, he has been careful to explain what his daughter Anansewa stands to gain from his design, but nobody has heard him making any direct hints about what he personally will gain. [*He shakes his head, smiling.*] Ananse! [*He pauses reflectively.*] Listen, I have a feeling that he has overdone it a little. It might well be that Anansewa was right to feel afraid.

The process which Ananse is exploiting to select a husband for his daughter, and at the same time as a means of getting maintenance for both of them, is full of snares. What if he cannot extricate himself? [*Listening*] I hear footsteps. Is someone coming?

[*He moves aside quickly.* POSTMAN *enters with a letter in his hand. He mimes checking the address on the letter against the address of a house in a street. He finds the house for which he is searching.*]

POSTMAN: Here is the address. AW/6615 Lagoon Street. It's correct. [*Testing the weight of the letter.*] This is a letter of some weight. [*He clears his throat.*] Is there someone to let me in?

STORYTELLER: [*To* POSTMAN:] I greet you.

POSTMAN: [*Approaching him:*] Are you house No. AW/6615?

STORYTELLER: Do I look like a house?

POSTMAN: I didn't mean that, sir. Didn't mean to offend. Are you Mr George K. Ananse of this address?

STORYTELLER: May that never be. [ANANSE *enters, a faraway look in his eyes.*] But I don't think the man you want has gone very far. He might be that man standing over there. [*He joins the* PLAYERS.]

POSTMAN: [*Signalling with the letter*] Sir!

ANANSE: Me?

POSTMAN: Are you house No. AW/6615 Lagoon Street?

ANANSE: [*Feebly*] That's right.

POSTMAN: Letter for Mr George K. Ananse.

ANANSE: [*He seizes the letter and studies it, turning it over. Happiness takes over.*] I say, Togbe Klu! [*To* POSTMAN:] It comes from Akate, does it?

POSTMAN: Seems like it.

ANANSE: (*With a dismissing toss of his head*] Very well, boy, received. Good morning.

POSTMAN: Right you are. [*He leaves.*]

ANANSE: [*Pleased with the contents of the letter*] Oh! Oh! Yes, that's the way it's done. A postal order worth ... [*He is thrilled.*] Oh! Oh! Not bad at all. Togbe Klu. Cactus, it's not bad at all. You have started to make your inner nature evident. This is just the way it's done. [*He hurries back home.*]

END OF ACT ONE

Act Two

STORYTELLER: So then, Ananse didn't toil in vain?

PLAYERS: No.

STORYTELLER: Still, isn't this the first sign of trouble?

PLAYERS: Well, we shall see.

STORYTELLER: All right, whatever the case may be, we may as well wish him luck. [*To the gong-player:*] Calling!

[*Gong rhythm. Two women rise, one starting off the song for the Mboguo.*]

MBOGUO

[*The two women share the song with the* PLAYERS. *They dance to it in a matronly way.* STORYTELLER *leads them in the dance to* PROPERTY MAN *who hands to one of them a girdle* with money tied in a huge knot in it. She ties it round her waist.* STORYTELLER *accompanies them back to sit in their places.*]

> Am I not Odum's† child?
>
> Am I not Odum's child?
>
> Oh I hate the sun!
>
> Abena‡ e,
>
> I'd rather be dead.

---

* girdle: usually a narrow band of cloth a woman uses to tie her skirt round her waist, sometimes made roomy enough to serve for a purse as well—a practice exaggerated in this play.

† Odum: name of a rich and powerful man in a folktale.

‡ Abena: daughter of Odum who got married and had not been prepared for the difficulties that she encountered.

Oh delicate one,

Abena e,
Abena e,
I'd rather be dead.

I never did toil,

Abena e,
Abena e,
I'd rather be dead.

Unseasoned one,

Abena e,
Abena e,
I'd rather be dead.

Oh pitiful one,

Abena e
Abena e
I'd rather be dead.

[PROPERTY MAN *sets a chair and a side table when the dance ends.* ANANSE, *dressed in a brand-new cloth, enters in good spirits and sits.*]

ANANSE: Serve my gin here.

[PROPERTY MAN *obliges. While* ANANSE *is sipping his gin the song ceases. Promptly, the two women rise in haste and keeping step with each other move towards* ANANSE. *They are* SAPAASE MESSENGERS *now.*]

SAPAASE MESSENGERS: [*Together*] Agoo!* We are looking for Pa Ananse.
FIRST MESSENGER: We were told he lived here.
ANANSE: I am Ananse.
SECOND MESSENGER: Is that so?
TOGETHER: [*Curtsying*] Oh, then good morning, Pa.
FIRST MESSENGER: We have been sent from Sapaase Palace.

* Agoo!: vocalised knocking.

ANANSE: [*With great fuss*] Chairs! Bring chairs for the messengers of royalty. [PROPERTY MAN *provides chairs.*] And water! Water, instantly! Let the royal travellers have water at once. [*Sitting down himself.*] You come from the great one himself, I know. All is well with us here.

SECOND MESSENGER: That is so.

FIRST MESSENGER: And, to be brief, he sends you greetings.

ANANSE: I respond.

[*The water drinking over, the woman with the girdle round her waist unties it.*]

MESSENGERS: And he asks us to place this money in your hands. He says, he is placing it in your hands so that if the object of his interest should need anything you will have the wherewithal. He wants you to understand that in doing this, he does not mean to say that he wants anything from you immediately. This is an outright gift. If other gifts follow afterwards, he knows you will understand that he is merely doing what it is beautiful to do until the time arrives.

[*The* MESSENGER *with the girdle unties the money and hands it to* ANANSE.]

ANANSE: [*Taking the money with trembling hands*] Oh, because I perfectly understand what he means, I thank him.

FIRST MESSENGER: All right. Then, Pa, that is what brought us here this morning.

ANANSE: Well done.

SECOND MESSENGER: And because we have some shopping to do before we return to Sapaase, we would like to be excused.

ANANSE: I understand. You are excused. [*The women rise together.*] Tell the Mighty-Tree-Of-Ancient-Origin that I greet him over and over again. Tell the Guardian-Of-The-Needy, my thanks in profusion.

MESSENGERS: Right. He will be told. [*They start the song 'Am I Not Odum's Child' again, dance back to their places and stop the music.*]

ANANSE: [*Hastily counting the money*] And how much has the Chief sent? [*He finishes checking.*] Oh considerable. [*He weighs it.*]

Substantial. Oh, son of the gods, Chief of Sapa, you too can display. [*He beckons to* PROPERTY MAN.] Come over here, man. Tomorrow is Sunday, isn't it? [PROPERTY MAN *nods agreement.*] And the first Sunday of the month, isn't it? [PROPERTY MAN *agrees.*] In that case, tomorrow I'm going to church. [*He speaks to rhythmic accompaniment from drum and gong:*]

> I'm heading for town on a buying spree.
> I'll be seen with the best of the spenders,
> And when I return expect me to bring
> The latest cloth in town,
> The latest suit in town.
>
> Yes, tomorrow, I go to church.
> To deposit with the best of the spenders.
>
> Those born on Sunday,
> Those born on Monday,
> Those born on Tuesday.
>
> Yes, tomorrow, I go to church
> To deposit with the best of the spenders.
>
> Those born on Wednesday—
>
> You'll see Kweku depositing
> Alongside the best of the spenders.

[*He beckons to* PROPERTY MAN *again.*]

Come over, man. Go to town and buy every kind of newspaper on the market. Search them for notices of all memorial services and select for me the one which promises to draw the biggest crowd.

> Ah, I'm heading for town on a buying spree.
> To purchase clothes for me.
>
> Yes, tomorrow, I go to church
> To deposit with the best of the spenders.
>
> Tomorrow I go to church,
> Tomorrow I go to church,
> Tomorrow I go to church.

[*He dances off.*]

MBOGUO

[*The* PLAYERS *start humming a church hymn.* PROPERTY MAN *sets a collection plate for a playful collection-giving mime. Seating himself beside it as the priest, he starts calling from 'Those Born on Sunday'. At each call some of the* PLAYERS *line up and walk in procession to deposit their collections. Some take off various mannerisms which are unseemly in a church but common enough. The mime over, the hymn is dropped abruptly, and the Mboguo is brought to an end with three energetic repetitions of 'Tomorrow I go to church'. Workmen enter:* CARPENTER, MASON *and* PAINTER, *each identified by the tool he is carrying.*]

CARPENTER: Countryman, are you sure this is the house? [*He examines the ceiling with a professional eye.*]

MASON: Ask me, and ask me again.

PAINTER: No mistake. Yet, I don't know whether to say the man doesn't match the house, or the house doesn't match the man. But we have come exactly where he directed us. [*He scans the walls.*]

MASON: As for us, why should we care whether it's the man who doesn't match the house, or the house which doesn't match the man? Work is what we're after, and there's plenty of it here, and moreover, he is offering it to us. [*He examines the floor.*]

CARPENTER: Plenty work. We'll be here for three weeks. Not a bad contract.

MASON: Three? Is something wrong with you? I say, five weeks.

PAINTER: Mason is right. We can't finish too quickly.

ALL: [*Posing stylishly together*] At all.

MASON: Look here, Carpenter, if you have found another place where they want to give you work after you've finished here, and that's the reason why you're in a hurry, finish your share quick, quick, and go.

ALL: [*Repeating the stylish pose*] At all. We can't finish too quickly. At all.

CARPENTER: (*Seeing* PROPERTY MAN) Are you the steward here? Mr Ananse called us here.

ALL THREE: [*Posing again*] We come for service.

[PROPERTY MAN *turns to meet* ANANSE *who is entering in a dressing-gown and sporting a cigar.*]

ANANSE: Ah! You have arrived, have you?

ALL: [*Posing*] Yes, sir.

ANANSE: Excellent. If you'll follow me round, I'll show you the work. Top priority is this leaking roof. That's you, Carpenter, so listen carefully; particularly in that corner there. Do your best to make us waterproof. Now, which is Mason? Yes, you with the trowel, of course. I'm ordering new floors in the bedrooms. You'll see in a minute what a shocking state they're in. Ah, you're the painter. Total painting. In all the rooms.

Follow me. Take a look round the whole house. Smart service is what I require. In the very near future, visitors of no mean station will start coming here to honour us. I give you the contract. Go at it with vigour. Other workers are coming, plumbers, electricians . . . [*He has led the way out of sight.*]

PAINTER: [*In a whisper to* MASON] Countryman, we've got the man in our pocket.

MASON: I'm telling you.

CARPENTER: Your five weeks is correct.

MASON: Shut your mouth. We're doubling it to ten weeks.

ANANSE: [*Off*] Where are you?

ALL: [*Repeating their pose*] Coming, sir!

MBOGUO

[*The workmen are earnestly at work. Hammering announces that* CARPENTER *is on the job somewhere. From time to time he crosses the stage energetically like a man with no time to spare.* MASON *and* PAINTER *are working on stage.* MASON *keeps calling out:* 'Concrete! Concrete!' PAINTER: 'Water! Water!' *They are supplied by* PROPERTY MAN. *It is* CARPENTER *who disrupts work after a while. He comes in to show his wrist watch to his friends who take his hint to quit and break off. Together, they dance stylishly towards the* PLAYERS *who have been singing their work songs with them, and sit among them.*]

First Song

Who doesn't like work?
Oh, I love work!

Work, work—

Who doesn't like work?
Oh, I love work!

Work, work—

This work that I do—

Yes, yes—

Supplies my clothing.

Yes, yes.

This work that I do—

Yes, yes—

Supplies my food.

Yes, yes.

This work that I do—

Yes, yes—

Supplies my cash.

Yes, yes.

Who doesn't like work?
Oh, I love work!

Work, work.

Second Song

I say, Kwabonyi,*
I'll never envy your wealth.

* Kwabonyi: name of a man.

> Kwabonyi, when you toil
> Do lift your head for he
> Who will spend it
> Sits idle somewhere.

[Before the second song ends, PROPERTY MAN sets a frame with a gorgeous curtain.]

STORYTELLER: I said so, oh I did. Ananse is not doing badly for himself. What he hinted at in a roundabout way is what is happening before our own eyes. There hasn't been any hitch in his plans so far. *[He reflects.]* I wonder if . . . if . . .

[The PLAYERS raise the song 'Kwabonyi' again. PROPERTY MAN brings in a lovely vase of flowers, and looks for a suitable place for it. Next, he brings in a beautiful garden chair and places it in front of the curtained frame, a little to the side. He appreciates the pleasant result. He tests the comfort of the chair.]

STORYTELLER: There before you is more evidence of what I was telling you. Oh, some time ago, it was bad at home, but maybe now it's getting better.

MBOGUO

[When STORYTELLER starts off the song, he falls luxuriously into the chair to try it. Several of the PLAYERS come dancing along in turn to follow suit. When they rise from the chair, they admire the general scene before dancing back to their places.]

> Oh, some time ago
> It was bad at home
> But maybe now it's getting better.
>
> Oh, some time ago
> It was bad at home
> But maybe now it's getting better.

Oh, friends, do look at Kweku Ananse's amazing ways.
It's with craftiness solely that he manages his life.

Oh, some time ago
It was bad at home
But maybe now it's getting better.

Oh, some time ago
It was bad at home
But maybe now it's getting better.

Oh, some time ago
It was bad at home
But maybe now it's getting better.

Oh, some time ago
It was bad at home
But maybe now it's getting better.

Oh, friends, do look at Kweku Ananse's cunning ways.
It's with falsehoods solely that he manages his life.

Oh, some time ago
It was bad at home
But maybe now it's getting better.

Oh, some time ago
It was bad at home
But maybe now it's getting better.

[*Before the song ends,* ANANSE *enters dressed in a suit fit for a business executive. His tie is a beauty.*]

ANANSE: If only things would stay as they are a little longer. But the time is running short on my daughter's affair. [*He sits in the garden chair, blowing his cheeks from the heat.*] Fellow, don't you realise how hot it is in the garden today? Bring me some ice-cream from the 'fridge. [PROPERTY MAN *serves him.*] Go on, you! Can't you sympathise with a man when you can see him getting hot under the collar? Fetch the electric fan out here to blow more breeze around me. [PROPERTY MAN *rushes to oblige.*] I must not permit events to take me by surprise.

[*As* PROPERTY MAN *manipulates a large toy electric fan beside him,* POSTMAN *enters.*]

POSTMAN: I was sure I was coming to the right house, but it's surely not the same. There ought to be a gate here, and . . .

ANANSE: Are you looking for me?

POSTMAN: No sir, I'm looking for Mr G. K. Ananse, sir. I thought this was AW/6615 Lagoon Street.

ANANSE: [*With a smile*] You didn't think wrong. I am he.

POSTMAN: [*He can't quite believe it*] Is that so? [*He salutes.*] I beg your pardon, sir. Here's your letter.

ANANSE: [*Smiling*] You see? They are beginning to salute me. They are calling me Sir. If only time would stand still for me. [*Becoming business-like.*] Well, what have we got this time? [*He opens the letter.*] Good Lord! Again? [*He is thrilled.*] Oh, they say, they say, but I'm seeing the truth for myself. Another cheque! Oh, you whose name is whispered in the ear, you are scoring goals.

This is your thirteenth cheque to arrive. And the largest amount you've ever sent. [*He sits.*] And yet, I'm not at all certain he is the one I would like to win the competition. Sitting as he does on mines of gold and diamonds, he can afford to let money keep flowing abundantly here. But what about his character? What kind of life will he lead my daughter? Oh, why doesn't Chief-Who-Is-Chief increase his pace a little more? He would save me from worrying so much. [*He shouts at* PROPERTY MAN.] Blow me some more breeze. [*He bows his head deep in thought.*]

CHIEF-WHO-IS-CHIEF'S MESSENGER: Can I come in?

ANANSE: [*He rises and stumbles over himself when he sees who has arrived.*] Do. Oh, my goodness, good afternoon!

CHIEF-WHO-IS-CHIEF'S MESSENGER: Good afternoon, sir. I've been sent here.

ANANSE: So I see. Take my chair.

CHIEF-WHO-IS-CHIEF'S MESSENGER: I'm talking to Mr George Ananse, I presume.

ANANSE: It's he indeed.

[MESSENGER *sits in the chair.* PROPERTY MAN *brings a chair for* ANANSE.]

Bring drinks.

CHIEF-WHO-IS-CHIEF'S MESSENGER: Don't bother, sir, if it's for me. I can't stay long because of having to be back in time for an important meeting.

ANANSE: Of course! Whatever you say.

CHIEF-WHO-IS-CHIEF'S MESSENGER: I see I need not tell you who sent me.

ANANSE: No, indeed. We know.

CHIEF-WHO-IS-CHIEF'S MESSENGER: Well. [*He clears his throat.*] Chief-Who-Is-Chief greets you, and greets er . . . the daughter?

ANANSE: Yes, yes, we understand perfectly.

CHIEF-WHO-IS-CHIEF'S MESSENGER: He says he is anxious not to cause you any kind of inconvenience . . .

ANANSE: Oh, we know that Chief-Who-Is-Chief is a most thoughtful man.

CHIEF-WHO-IS-CHIEF'S MESSENGER: So he is letting you know in good time that er . . . it won't be very long before er . . . he will be completing the preparations for sending people er . . . to come and er . . .

ANANSE: [*Almost plucking the words off the man's lips*] I'm all ears.

CHIEF-WHO-IS-CHIEF'S MESSENGER: I mean that people will come to place on the table for you, the head-drink for the lady, your daughter.

ANANSE: Delicious news! Cut a little whisky with me, Mr Honourable. Hey, bring the drinks! [PROPERTY MAN *serves. Glasses are raised.*] Sweet news, Mr Honourable. [*They drink.*] Did he specify the day?

CHIEF-WHO-IS-CHIEF'S MESSENGER: Oh, yes. Two weeks today.

[ANANSE *pauses for a quick calculation.*]

ANANSE: That's fine! [*He is reflective but happy.*]

CHIEF-WHO-IS-CHIEF'S MESSENGER: Er . . . I do have to be on my way back, sir, so if you'll excuse me . . .

ANANSE: Oh, you're certainly excused. Thanks for your great news. [*He walks a little way with him.*] Do drive with care. Go well. [*He becomes reflective again.*]

[*As* MESSENGER *bows out, he collides with* POSTMAN.]

POSTMAN: Oh, sorry, sir. [*He stares curiously at the departing guest.*]

ANANSE: Are you back again?

POSTMAN: You see, sir? Some days it's to and fro all day long. Telegram, sir.

ANANSE: From where?

POSTMAN: I'm not supposed to know, sir.

[ANANSE *signs for the telegram and returns the receipt.*]

Goodbye, sir.

ANANSE: Take this for some cigarettes. [*He takes out money.*]

POSTMAN: [*Eager to take it*] Oh, sir, never mind.

ANANSE: Oh, take it, for I'm happy beyond description.

POSTMAN: Thank you, sir. God bless you. [*He bows out.*]

ANANSE: He has blessed me in a most amazing way.

[*When he tears the telegram open, and reads it, he sinks into the chair with his eyes popping, and blows his cheeks.*]

Hey, fellow, blow me some breeze.

[PROPERTY MAN *turns the fan faster.*]

What am I going to do? In such a fix, what am I going to do? (*He reads the telegram again aloud.*] 'Announcing messengers' arrival to conduct head-drink ceremony for Anansewa after two weeks stop greetings stop Chief Sapa.' Oh spirits, what shall I do? [*Turning on* PROPERTY MAN] Hey, haven't you any sympathy for a man hit by a storm? Cut off the breeze.

[*He sits thinking with his jaws agape.* PROPERTY MAN *brings in a spider web screen and screens him off.*]

MBOGUO

[STORYTELLER *approaches the web, stands in front of it and calls playfully to* ANANSE.]

STORYTELLER: Ananse,

Ananse Ekuamoa,
Man-is-cunning Ananse!

His mind is far away. It's as if he weren't with us here.

Ananse!
George!
George Kweku!
Sir!

He has retreated far, far away. He is nowhere near us. Whatever is it that could bring him back? A song?

[STORYTELLER, ANANSE *and* PLAYERS *share a song*.]

Who is knocking?
Who is knocking?

It's me.
It's me.

Who is knocking?
When I'm thinking?

It's me.
It's me.

I'm ailing,
I'm ailing.

It's me. ·
It's me.

Stop disturbing,
Stop disturbing.

It's me.
It's me.

ANANSE: Ah, my head! Who's that knocking to disturb me?
STORYTELLER: It's me!
ANANSE: Oh, stop disturbing,
                     Stop disturbing.

> Ah, the world is hard,
> Is hard,
> The world is really hard.

[*He groans and rises. The spying* STORYTELLER *retreats in a hurry from the web to join the* PLAYERS.]

STORYTELLER: He is coming.

[ANANSE *cautiously draws the web screen aside and steps out from behind it. The* PLAYERS *continue the song softly.*]

ANANSE: [*Calling* PROPERTY MAN:] Man, I need a headache pill. Don't you have any sympathy for a man struck by an earthquake of a headache? [PROPERTY MAN *helps him to take a pill. The singing gets louder.*] Look, that song of yours is disturbing me, I say. [*The singing gets soft again.*] Listen, man, to what I want you to do for me. It's become necessary for Anansewa to return home at once. Telephone Tarkwa 30, to the Institute For Prospective Brides and say that at seven thirty tonight I will speak to Miss Christina Yamoah.

[*The* PLAYERS *sing loudly again.* ANANSE *stuffs his ears with his fingers with irritation and takes to flight.* PROPERTY MAN *mimes telephoning vigorously. The song ends with his act.*]

END OF ACT TWO

Act Three

[*Enter* AYA, ANANSE's *mother. She is very well dressed in grand-motherly style, looking as though she has stepped out of an old photograph.*]

AYA: I can't understand my son Ananse at all. Why does he want an outdooring ceremony for Anansewa all of a sudden? You school people say you have thrown these things aside. Very well, throw them aside. But to wait until five years after the girl has become a woman, and then say 'outdoor her'! That's not good custom-keeping in anybody's world.

[*Enter* EKUWA, ANANSE's *aunt.*]

EKUWA: Mm, Aya, are you already here? I see you are keeping your eyes wide open to make sure that nothing goes wrong with your grandchild Anansewa's outdooring. Sit down, we'll be bringing her outdoors in just a few more minutes.

[*She turns for a stool from* PROPERTY MAN, *and bending sideways, gives the finishing touches to* AYA's *dress.*]

AYA: I'm saying that I can't see why Kweku is doing this at all. If the time for doing something passes by, it has passed by.

EKUWA: Ah, Aya. I've been trying very hard to explain it to you. If this grandchild of yours is going to marry a chief, then it is our duty to prepare her in every way we can for the position she will be occupying in a palace.

AYA: All right. Whatever it may be, I'm happy to see my Anansewa conducting herself in the manner that graces a woman. You don't know what feelings are breaking and ebbing like waves inside me because of this ceremony we are performing. This wave brings happiness, that one brings pride, and another, sadness. Yes, it is true that you and I are here doing all we can, and yet when I remember that the person who should be here as well, bustling around Anansewa, is her own mother, then, my sister Ekuwa, a wave of sorrow crests up inside me, mangling my innards. [*She starts to dirge.*] And it isn't as though she is where we could send her a telegram to say, 'come'. It isn't as though we could send a messenger by taxi to fetch her. [*She is about to wail seriously.*] Truly, death has done some wickedness.

EKUWA: [*Quickly*] Aya, I'm on my knees to you, don't start doing that at all. I don't believe you want to ruin Anansewa's joy.

AYA: [*Desisting*] Is my grandchild Anansewa enjoying what we're doing for her? Does she like this outdooring of hers?

EKUWA: She is enjoying it so much, I'm surprised. She keeps on asking questions in order to learn as much as she can.

AYA: Very well. And where is that woman?

EKUWA: Auntie Christina Yamoah? She is dressing our child. She has nearly finished dressing her hair.

AYA: Tell her she mustn't ruin my grandchild with too much fanciful dressing. The woman is senselessly extravagant.

[CHRISTIE, *rushing past, notices them there. She is* MISS CHRISTINA YAMOAH, *a fashionable woman.*]

CHRISTIE: [*Dabbing her face with her handkerchief*] Ah, mother, are you seated already? Anansewa is ready. How I've dressed up my daughter! Oh, I nearly forgot . . . [*She dashes out.*]

AYA: Ekuwa.

EKUWA: Aya.

AYA: You see that woman?

EKUWA: Yes.

AYA: I'm telling you today, for your information, that she is serving my son Kweku too hard.

EKUWA: Do you think so?

AYA: 'I've dressed up my daughter Anansewa', indeed! When did my grandchild become her daughter? And also, whom is she calling mother? Me?

EKUWA: Aya, she is just trying to be helpful. Because our child is in

training with her, Kweku specially invited her to come and
help, and she came.

AYA: [*Snorting*] The way I see it, she is leaning her ladder on my
grandchild in order to climb up to my son.

[GIRLS *raise their song in the distance.*]

EKUWA: There's no time now for us to discuss her. That's Anansewa's friends coming over to bring her out. Won't you let us
meet them with joy?

[*She snatches up her stole, meets the* GIRLS *as they enter, and crosses
through with them.*]

> Aba* e,
> We've come to perform.
> Aba e,
> We've come to perform.
> Let it be perfect,
>
> A gift from God.
>
> We've come to perform.
> Let it be perfect,
>
> A child from God.
>
> We've come to perform.
> Let it be perfect.
>
> Aba e,
> We've come to perform.
> Aba e,
> We've come to perform.
> Let it be perfect,
>
> Blessing from God.
>
> We've come to perform.
> Let it be perfect.

* Aba: approximately, 'We're on our way; here we come.'

> Aba e,
> We've come to perform.
> Aba e,
> We've come to perform.
> Let it be perfect.

AYA: Ah, bring out my precious bead. My *bota** bead, my gold child.

[PROPERTY MAN *places* ANANSEWA'*s chair. The* GIRLS *raise their song again and bring her out, carrying her gracefully, preventing her feet from touching the ground. A veil covers her face.* AYA *sits down and waits for the song to end.*]

AYA: [*Rising*] Anansewa, my grandchild, it is what we know to be beautiful that we are doing for you. Today, this old lady will really dance. She will dance. Calling! [*Gong rhythm begins. She starts off the song.*]

> My Anansewa,
> Oho!
>
> Pure gold gracing her,
> Oho!
>
> Sandals gracing her,
> Oho!
>
> Honour gracing her,
> Oho!
>
> Courting her, they rail at me,
> Courting her, they rail at me.
> When I bear a child with her
> They nurse it on their backs.

[*Speaking:*] At the very crack of dawn, we cleansed you. We clipped your nails, we shaved you. With new sponge and new soap, and with life-giving water, we bathed you. Today, this old lady will dance. Calling! [*Gong rhythm.*]

---

* *bota*: one of the most famous and precious of beads, known as the Aggrey bead.

ANANSE: Yes, tomorrow I go to church
To deposit with the best of the spenders.

ANANSEWA: 'Anansewa, it is what we know
to be beautiful that we are doing for you.'

> Courting her, they rail at me
> Courting her, they rail at me
> When I bear a child with her
> They nurse it on their backs.

[*Speaking:*] We squeezed lime on your head to season you, so that when life's hardships approach, you will be capable of standing firm to field them. Oh, my! It's because we're doing things right that this old lady is dancing, Anansewa. Calling! [*Gong rhythm.*]

> Courting her, they rail at me
> Courting her, they rail at me
> When I bear a child with her
> They nurse it on their backs.

[*Speaking:*] Ah, Anansewa, my grandchild, in your name, we have sprinkled sacred palm-oiled yam. We have touched your lips with an egg to invoke blessings for you, and we have adorned you with gold to honour you. Oh, my! Let the old lady step it out, do. Calling! [*Gong rhythm.*]

> Courting her, they rail at me
> Courting her, they rail at me
> When I bear a child with her
> They nurse it on their backs.

[*Speaking:*] Oh listen, everyone. This day, I am declaring to the public, that what we know to be beautiful, we have done for this child of ours.

GIRLS: Well done. And you have done it perfectly.

[*They unveil* ANANSEWA.]

EKUWA: Ah, here's a lovely thing. Oh, let me give service to my child. Man, give me my child's brass bowl. [*She runs to receive it, half filled with water, from* PROPERTY MAN, *and places it in public view.*] Anansewa, it's for you I'm spending my energy. [*She returns for nyanya leaves.*] Sir, give me the *nyanya,** please.

---

* *nyanya*: a vine used in ritual ceremonies, believed to have the power to purge and avert evil forces, and to purify.

Anansewa, my child of beauty, we are doing it, and doing some more. [*She drops the leaves in the water.*] Sir, now give me the egg for my child's soul. [*She gets it.*] Anansewa, look, here is your soul's egg. I place it before you. May it attract good fortune for you.

[*She places it in front of* ANANSEWA. *Enter* CHRISTIE. *She walks daintily over to stand beside the brass bowl.* PROPERTY MAN *places something in her outstretched hand.*]

CHRISTIE: I will be the first to place my gift in this brass bowl. Anansewa, my darling, I never thought I would part with this sovereign in my hand. And yet, you see what love's power can do? When Georgie told me you were to be outdoored, I nearly went mad with joy. I asked myself, 'What on earth shall I give Anansewa, my sweetie?' I said, I'll give her something I value. Therefore, here is this sovereign which is so precious to me. Take it, it's yours, my dear. Things go where they belong. It is not as though I were throwing it away on some stranger.

[*She drops the coin into the water and walks back without noticing* AYA'*s disapproving face. She takes a position directly behind* ANANSEWA. EKUWA *picks up the egg, and passes it over* ANANSEWA'*s head with an arching gesture.* CHRISTIE *receives it and places it right behind* ANANSEWA. *Some of the* GIRLS *now give their gifts.*]

GIRLS: [*Taking turns*] Anansewa, you are now ready to marry.
Anansewa, you will give birth to thirty.
Anansewa, may your life be healthy.

[*When each one places her gift in the brass bowl, or beside* ANANSEWA, EKUWA *and* CHRISTIE *see to it that the egg is passed over from one side to the other. As soon as the last girl has made her statement, the* GIRLS *break into song and surge round* ANANSEWA *in dance.*]

Sensemise* e
We welcome you this day.
Sensemise e
We welcome you this day.
Sensemise e
Welcome to you.

Anansewa,
We welcome you this day.
Anansewa,
We welcome you this day.

Anansewa,
Oh, welcome to you,
Anansewa,
We welcome you this day,
Anansewa,
Oh, welcome to you.

AYA: Now, quiet everyone; and let me make my statement. Where is my son?

CHRISTIE: [*Walking off with great fuss*] Georgie! Georgie! Mother is calling you.

AYA: [*Staring in disapproval but controlling herself*] This would not normally be a time when men mix with us. But I do want my son to stand here while I give my gift to this grandchild of mine. [*Calling him herself:*] Kweku!

[ANANSE *enters,* CHRISTIE *holding his hand.*]

ANANSE: Am I wanted among the women?

CHRISTIE: Yes, your mother wants you.

ANANSE: I'm here, mother.

AYA: Lady, if you can manage it, let go of my son's hand for a while. [CHRISTIE *releases her hold and returns to her place.*] Kweku, come close to this brass bowl and listen. My grandchild Anansewa, your old lady knows something about what is of real value in this world. You notice that this outstretched hand of mine is empty, it contains nothing. And yet, this same empty

* Sensemise: a refrain word expressing a sense of joy.

41

hand will succeed in placing a gift into your brass bowl. What this hand is offering is this prayer of mine. May the man who comes to take you from our hands to his home be, above all things, a person with respect for the life of his fellow human beings; a man who is incapable of . . .

ANANSE: [*Anxious to prevent whatever follows from being said, he bursts forth with exaggerated joy.*] Hey. She is speaking! She is speaking! Old lady is speaking! Girls, get your throats vibrating! [*He himself starts singing and dancing.*]

> Sensemise e
> We welcome you this day.

[*He gets the help he desires from the* GIRLS. *Singing and dancing takes over.*]

EKUWA: We have finished. We are taking our girl away.

[*Taking up their song again, the* GIRLS *carry* ANANSEWA *back, accompanied by* AYA *and* EKUWA. ANANSE *is still dancing when* POSTMAN *arrives.*]

POSTMAN: Oh sir, are you dancing?
ANANSE: Hello, there. Do you bring sweet news?
POSTMAN: Ah, sir, if God wishes it so. Here's a telegram. It comes from . . .
ANANSE: Yes, my detective. Tell me everything about it, then. Tell me from where, and from whom it comes, and the message it contains.

[POSTMAN *hangs his head in embarrassment.* ANANSE *signs for the telegram and returns the receipt. Left alone, he reads it, and what he reads pleases him so much that he reads it aloud.*]

'Anansewa's ceremony makes your wisdom evident stop well-done for furthering her education in this manner stop. [*He frowns.*] Appropriate this day to declare my thoughts to you that . . . [ANANSE *gets stuck.*] That, that, . . .' [*When he speaks again he is nasal.*] Oh, where am I going to turn? '. . . that not wanting to waste any more time I am coming to present the head-drink for her stop Togbe Klu.' [*He calls:*] Christie! Christie!

CHRISTIE: [*Rushing*] George, what's wrong with you?

ANANSE: Christie, my head aches.

CHRISTIE: [*To* PROPERTY MAN:] Bring aspirin or anything to stop a headache. Man, hurry.

ANANSE: All of a sudden, an earthquake has erupted in my head. [*He takes the pill from* CHRISTIE.] Haven't you finished with the ceremony? See to bringing it quickly to an end.

CHRISTIE: [*Getting him water for taking the pill*] But George, where does a sudden headache like this come from?

ANANSE: There's no time for questions. See to dispatching the guests, because I'm anxious for silence in this house. It's become necessary for me to think.

CHRISTIE: [*Puzzled*] All right, George, the house will quieten down for you. I'll do whatever gives you pleasure. [*On her way out she remembers something and whistles.*] Oh, George! Goodness, if I overlook things in this manner, how do I apologise?

[*She turns back and takes a telegram from* PROPERTY MAN, *but the* GIRLS *interrupt her as they come through singing and dancing.*]

GIRLS: Stay away from that town,
                   Never go down there.
                   Stay away from that town,
                   Never go down, down there.

                   It's a town where cripples
                   Climb into your bed, bed, bed.

                   Stay away from that town,
                   Never go down, down there.

[*Halting briefly*] Bye bye, daddy!

[ANANSE *fakes a smiling face and waves back at them.*]

Bye bye, Auntie Christie!

CHRISTIE: Bye bye, slender threads. [*When they have passed through, she gives the telegram to* ANANSE.] Listen, this telegram was brought, just this afternoon. It's yours. Do you know where it comes from? And I was idiotic enough to forget it. Believe me, it was because we were so busy that it escaped my mind. George will forgive Christie, won't he? [ANANSE *turns the telegram over and over without opening it.*] Won't you read it? It comes from the Mines. Do you know, Georgie, up to this day you don't tell me precisely what is engaging you, so that I'll be informed. I had no idea we have now turned our attention to the Mines people. I was thinking that our attention was strongly concentrated on Chief-Who-Is-Chief. [ANANSE *is dazed and still turning the telegram over and over.*] Won't you read it?

ANANSE: [*Irritably*] Stop, Christie. I've told you I want it quiet here. Even you will have to be quiet. Hm.

CHRISTIE: [*Embarrassed*] Really? All right. [*She leaves him alone.*]

ANANSE: [*He opens the telegram and reads it aloud.*] 'The day after tomorrow I am sending to . . .' [*His jaw drops. He is nasal when he speaks again.*] Just the day after tomorrow?

[PROPERTY MAN *places a web screen.* ANANSE *drags himself backwards to hide behind it.* ANANSEWA *enters.*]

ANANSEWA: I never imagined that this ceremony would touch me so much. I have a lovely feeling inside my heart. [*She re-enacts parts of the ceremony close to where her father is hiding.*]

'Anansewa, you are a woman now. Anansewa, it is what we know to be beautiful that we are doing for you. We have touched your lips with an egg to bless you, and we have dressed you in gold to honour you.'

[*She mimes the passing of the egg.*]

'Good fortune accompany you always.'

[*She sings 'Sensemise' and dances round for a while.*]

But where is father? Father! Father, where are you? [*She catches sight of him, watching her from behind the screen, and is startled.*]

Oh father, is that you? But why has your manner changed so?

[ANANSE *pops out and stands beside the web.*]

Why do you seem so far away?

[ANANSE *doesn't reply.*]

I want to tell you what a lovely feeling I have inside me, and thank you.

ANANSE: [*Staring fixedly at her*] My daughter.

ANANSEWA: Father.

ANANSE: Are you happy?

[*The expression on his face alarms* ANANSEWA.]

ANANSEWA: I thought I was happy.

ANANSE: Why do you say you *thought*? What makes you think you are not happy now?

ANANSEWA: I can't think what it is.

ANANSE: [*Sighing*] The world is puzzling,
                    Is puzzling,
                    The world is really puzzling.

ANANSEWA: Father, don't talk so sadly on such a day, please.

ANANSE: My daughter.

ANANSEWA: Father.

ANANSE: Are you well?

ANANSEWA: [*Emphatically*] Yes!

ANANSE: You believe that?

ANANSEWA: [*Now very uneasy*] Oh, I thought I was well. Oh, why has my mind become so confused?

[*She hasn't noticed it, but* PROPERTY MAN *has placed a web screen right behind her.*]

Now, I don't know if I'm well and happy, or if I'm not well, and unhappy too.

ANANSE: [*Darting closer to her*] Open your eyes wide, and let me see.

ANANSEWA: What? Very well, I've opened them.

45

ANANSE: [*Peering into her eyes*] Shut them tight.

ANANSEWA: [*Smiling a little and obliging*] I've shut them tight.

ANANSE: Mhm. Stiffen your limbs.

ANANSEWA: [*Opening her eyes*] For what reason? [*She laughs.*] Very well, I have stiffened my limbs. [*She does so.*]

ANANSE: Do it properly. I want you to look as though you are dead.

ANANSEWA: What do you mean? [*She laughs.*] I have never died before.

ANANSE: My daughter, I implore you, don't waste time. What I'm doing is in serious preparation.

ANANSEWA: [*Understanding nothing at all*] Preparation?

ANANSE: Yes, my daughter, stiffen yourself.

ANANSEWA: [*Doing so with laughter*] There you are. Are you satisfied?

ANANSE: [*Very pleased*] It's really coming right. Try not to move any part of your body. [ANANSEWA *tries.*] Oh yes, it's really coming right. And now, can't you stop breathing a little? Can't you hold your breath?

ANANSEWA: [*Finding this too much*] Hold my breath! I shouldn't breathe? As for that, definitely no, I can't do it, and will not.

ANANSE: Oh, but my daughter, it's necessary for you to die!

ANANSEWA: Me? [*Words fail her.*] But father, I'm alive. I'm open-eyed. How can I switch my life off and on like electricity?

ANANSE: Don't spout silly jokes, you don't understand what we are doing.

ANANSEWA: Then make me understand; because this game you're playing is full of mystery. I don't like it.

ANANSE: My daughter.

ANANSEWA: Father.

ANANSE: You are forcing me to tell you that those four people are coming. Just coming? They are rushing here. Sprinting.

ANANSEWA: Who?

ANANSE: Oh, dear! Who else but the four chiefs? [ANANSEWA *is still in the dark.*] They are racing here like fire blazing through grass.

ANANSEWA: What four chiefs are racing here?

ANANSE: Oh-h-h, dear! Rouse your memory if it's asleep, and

remember. I tell you there is no time to waste. Each chief's messengers are on their way, urgently sent to place your head-drink on the table.

ANANSEWA: [*Exploding with laughter*] And how does such a situation become possible?

ANANSE: It is possible, my child. It is seriously possible.

ANANSEWA: It's not one bit possible; so why are you insisting it is?

ANANSE: Look at how we are standing here wasting time. Anansewa, if I say it's possible, believe me. I tell you that each chief is coming running to claim you as his wife.

ANANSEWA: [*Laughing*] Over my dead body.

ANANSE: [*Starting*] Ah, young lady, how clever you are. Is it some spirit which inspired you to say that?

ANANSEWA: I repeat, over my dead body. How can they claim me as their own? [*Laughter chokes her.*] They are coming to claim me as their own indeed! They dare not.

ANANSE: [*Distressed*] If I were you, I wouldn't say so emphatically that they dare not. Why can't they dare? They can dare.

ANANSEWA: Father, why? All that aside, why do you say 'they'? Why don't you say 'he', the single one?

ANANSE: [*His eyes darting*] Are you asking me why?

ANANSEWA: Yes, why? Because I know that it's only one chief we are expecting to come. And as far as that person is concerned, he cannot come too quickly for me. I'm waiting for him asleep and awake. As for the other three chiefs, my father, you made them take their minds off me long ago, remember. Right at the beginning, you refused to accept gifts from their hands.

ANANSE: [*Groaning*] Ah, children! Ah! Children are so pathetic. Anansewa, that's not all there is to this affair.

ANANSEWA: Well, you did deliver me from their hands, didn't you? As far as they are concerned, didn't the affair become a case of no-sale-no-payment? [*She thinks this very funny.*]

ANANSE: Such childishness. What does one do to make children understand that the ways of the world are complicated?

ANANSEWA: [*Realisation dawning on her*] Father!

ANANSE: [*Tired*] My daughter. You are calling me 'father' to say you have compassion for me, aren't you?

ANANSEWA: [*Ready to flare up*] I am calling you father to tell you

47

that if what has happened is that you've been telling me a lie, I'll be deeply shocked.

ANANSE: [*Harassed*] Look, Anansewa, don't torture me, or I'll stop killing my brains in your interest. I myself will die instead, and leave you to your own desires in this wicked world. What is it you're calling a lie in this crazy world?

ANANSEWA: [*Out of control*] I don't know anything about the world . . .

ANANSE: Indeed you don't. You needn't declare it.

ANANSEWA: What I know is that you are my father, you asked me to trust you. You asked me to leave the four chiefs situation in your hands for you to disentangle.

ANANSE: Yes, I did say so. I asked you to trust me.

ANANSEWA: Thereafter, you told me emphatically that all was going well, the way it should.

ANANSE: I did. Oh, the world is hard.

ANANSEWA: And after that, why did you send me to the Institute for Prospective Brides?

ANANSE: [*Unable to stand it any longer*] I sent you there to place you far, far away from the range of young men's rampaging eyes, to get prepared for marriage.

ANANSEWA: In that case, my memory is not asleep. I clearly remember that when I was going away, you were absolutely sure there was one man alone for whose sake you were sending me there to get prepared.

ANANSE: [*With cunning*] I had no idea I was doing wrong. And now, see how things have turned against me. I've wearied myself for you in vain. I've spent sums of money on you in vain; and further, the interest of somebody's son has blazed in you in vain. I'm tremendously sorry to realise you don't love the man after all.

ANANSEWA: [*Pained*] But father, why are you confusing me like this? I, Anansewa, I don't love Chief-Who-Is-Chief? [*Her tears are close.*] Now I see what has happened. [*She is scared.*] Have you, by any chance, gone to Chief-Who-Is-Chief, and told him that I don't love him, and ruined everything? [*Cunning laughter from* ANANSE.] He has gone and told him that. Oh, the whole affair has ended. It's turned to wind. He has finished me. [*She breaks into song.*]

My heart, my heart,
Stop beating,
My heart, my heart.
The chance has turned to wind,
To wind, wind, wind.

Oh, Anansewa,
Oh, Anansewa,
Oh, Anansewa,
Anansewa, Anansewa.

My heart, my heart,
You're lonely,
My heart, my heart.
The chance has turned to wind
To wind, wind, wind.

ANANSE: I'm amazed that you can sing such a soulful love-song when you are not willing to do what you must do to get the man for a husband.

ANANSEWA: You mean that I am not willing to do what I must do to get Chief-Who-Is-Chief? I don't know what to think any longer now. You have confused me completely.

ANANSE: What I mean is that the chance has not turned to any 'wind, wind, wind'. Be willing to think with me; help me to implement what I have planned. Yes, discipline yourself and do what it has become necessary to do, and see if you don't get the man you say you love.

ANANSEWA: Why didn't you say that straightaway? Tell me quickly what it is that I must do. Say it, and stop my heart from breaking. I'm ready. [*She has moved until she is right behind the web screen by now.*]

ANANSE: Are you wholeheartedly, or only half heartedly ready?

ANANSEWA: From head to toe, I'm ready.

ANANSE: [*Grasping her hand happily*] Ah, how greatly relieved I am. I'm worn out.

[*He leads her by the hand to step out from behind the web, and whispers in her ear as if he is briefing her.* ANANSEWA *nestles her head on his shoulder. Enter* CHRISTIE.]

49

CHRISTIE: [*Coming upon them*] Georgie! Ah, such a lovely sight! The one-and-only and her father sharing their secrets. That's just as it should be. [*Moving closer, she notices* ANANSEWA'S *troubled face.*] Anansewa, darling! Ho, my child, what's worrying you; anger or what? George, have you done something wrong? Darling, don't mind him, eh? Ah George, what's wrong with her?

ANANSE: Christie, I need help.

CHRISTIE: Then here I am, aren't I? Command me.

ANANSE: Anansewa is a child.

CHRISTIE: No doubt about that. She is a baby at the breast.

ANANSE: You and I must do our best to explain to her a bit about the nature of life's entanglements.

CHRISTIE: Thank you for saying you and me. My child, will you permit Auntie Christie and Dada dear to help you understand a few things?

[ANANSEWA *slips away from* ANANSE *to take refuge in* CHRISTIE'S *bosom.*]

You see? She will permit us.

AYA: [*Coming upon them*] If someone else were me, she would ask the reason for this talking in whispers with your heads in a huddle. Kweku, I want you people to release my daughter to me so that I can feed her. Come, my grandchild.

[ANANSEWA *flies into her arms, and* AYA *takes her precious one away.*]

CHRISTIE: Georgie, whatever it is that is worrying you and affecting Anansewa on such a day, why don't you tell me?

ANANSE: Christie, I must do something fast, or else a roaring fire that is racing here will consume me.

CHRISTIE: Take the veil off whatever the trouble is and inform me so that I'll understand. Once I know what kind of trouble it is, I can help.

ANANSE: My mother and aunt should leave. They are leaving for Nanka immediately.

CHRISTIE: So suddenly?

ANANSE: Immediately. They must not stay here to see what it has become necessary for me to do, because they won't understand. They'll be scared.

CHRISTIE: [*She doesn't understand*] Well, perhaps I'll understand in due course.

ANANSE: [*In a daze*] This very night, I must begin the task. I must do everything in my power to untie the knot I tied myself. I've got to succeed in untying it, or else . . . it will be disastrous for me.

CHRISTIE: [*Uneasy*] George, George. [ANANSE *starts.*] What do you wish me to do? Name it. Say it.

ANANSE: Go and make arrangements for a taxi to take my mother and aunt away. Don't waste any time bargaining on the price.

CHRISTIE: [*On her way*] I must say that this hot haste is truly mysterious.

ANANSE: Go, Christie.

CHRISTIE: George, darling, easy. I'm going.

ANANSE: [*His mind off* CHRISTIE] And I am going to see my mother and aunt and find a way by which to give them a hint about their departure.

CHRISTIE [*To herself*] Why doesn't he tell me what the trouble is? Well, here I go. This man George! For how long am I going to serve him before I get him? Oh Georgie!

ANANSE: [*Roused by his name*] Yes?

CHRISTIE: [*Embarrassed at the thought that she has been overheard*] I called you, did I? Oh, George, I wasn't even aware I did. As for your name, it's always on my lips.

[*She leaves.* ANANSE *watches her until she's out of sight and laughs.*]

ANANSE: I know that Christie happens to be an experienced, worldly-wise woman. I know she is capable of helping me to do what I have planned. Mother and aunt are another matter. Whatever can I tell them to induce them to depart? Oh, my head!

[*In his distress he talks to the world at large.*]

Do you see what is happening to me? Very well, look at how

I'm cornered, and if you so desire, laugh at me. It's no one else's fault but mine that no fewer than four chiefs are invading me to claim my one daughter, and terrifying me into this state.

But let me tell you this: if you are merely human like me, you'd better make your laughter brief, because in this world, there is nobody who is by-passed by trouble.

[*He holds out his hand for a handkerchief from* PROPERTY MAN, *and sobs into it.*]

> The world is hard,
> The world is hard,
> The world is really hard.

AYA: [*Entering to find him in this state*] My son, is this weeping you're weeping? What's the matter?

ANANSE: [*Wringing out the handkerchief*] Mother!

AYA: My stalwart son.

ANANSE: Mother. [*He returns the handkerchief, and acting like a man in conflict, yells out:*] Destroyers! Evil-doers! They won't rest until they have ruined me. Enemies whose outward appearance makes you think they are not enemies.

AYA: [*Wide-eyed with confusion*] Enemies? It's that woman Christie, isn't it? The minute I met that woman here I felt instinctively that trouble marches alongside people of her kind.

ANANSE: [*Bursting into tears afresh*] Handkerchief!

[PROPERTY MAN *supplies him again.*]

AYA: [*Completely lost*] Stop, Kweku. [*She calls out:*] Ekuwa! Run over here, Kweku is crying. My son, have I said something bad?

ANANSE: Instead of packing up your things promptly and going where my enemies are to fight them for me, you stand there uselessly—and falsely—blaming poor Christie.

AYA: I apologise, I shouldn't have said that. Drop it. Ekuwa! Come and help me to apologise to Kweku.

ANANSE: It isn't any apology that will help me. It is necessary for you to return home, because it's there the trouble has occurred.

AYA: Home?

ANANSE: Yes. Our home-town Nanka itself. Someone has just

reported to me that . . . that enemies have set fire to our hope. Our cocoa farm.

AYA: What, the cocoa? Ekuwa!

ANANSE: There is the telephone; still tingling with the news.

EKUWA: [*Tidying herself up as she enters*] I heard a call for me. What's the matter? I heard someone saying 'cocoa'.

ANANSE: My capital which I invested in our family land is all ruined. All those lovely cocoa trees, wasted. They say that flames are raging through them.

AYA: Ekuwa, they have finished us!

EKUWA: Didn't I say so? Did I not turn prophet and prophesy that as soon as the people of Nanka see a little improvement in our circumstances, skin-pain will seize them?

ANANSE: [*Suffering*] People are bad! [*He moves close to the web and watches from there.*]

AYA: People of Nanka! I'm going into reverse for you to watch and rejoice. My clothes are going to fade again, my blouse will get ragged enough for my breasts to flap through to give you reason to mock me. I knew it would not satisfy you if I didn't remain in rags to the end of my life.

ANANSE: People are bad!

EKUWA: People of Nanka! Laugh with satisfaction, then. Kweku's car will no longer arrive in Nanka and park outside the house of the Nsona clan.* Our hope having burnt down to ashes, how is he going to afford spare parts and petrol and tyres? You who have successfully lamed and ruined him, rejoice then. Pound *fufu* and eat it served with chicken groundnut soup in happy celebration of this victory of yours.

AYA: I am already an old woman. I'm abandoning myself for death to take me away.

ANANSE: Mother, don't die to give our enemies greater joy.

EKUWA: My sister with whom I come from the same nest, don't leave me behind. We will link our wings and suffer this adversity together. [*She ties her top cloth† to* AYA*'s.*] Kweku, if your mother goes, I follow her. Should I sit alone in the courtyard of the Nsona clan house to suffer mockery from the tongues of Nanka citizens? I couldn't.

---

* Nsona clan: one of a number of principal clans.

† top cloth: a two-yard piece of cloth used as a stole.

ANANSE: How miserable I am. There's no lack of people who will weep for me. But as for people who will rise and get going to deal with my troubles, I haven't got a single one. Ah! Has the Nsona spirit become so weak that these days any hunchback may kick us with impunity?

AYA: [*Stung by the comment into great self-assertion*] Who said so? Who said our spirit is maimed? While I breathe? My son, you have said it right, I will not die to give our enemies greater joy. I will not hear news of this nature and sleep on it here tonight. I will not allow the wicked ones, whoever they are, to sleep in peace tonight. What! Ekuwa, I'm off at once to Nanka to sweep up these offspring of vipers and punish them.

EKUWA: I'm going with you. Cheer up, Kweku, we are not dead yet. [*They rush away, linked by their cloths.*]

ANANSE: [*Moving away from the web*] Listen, a taxi will soon be here to take you. Hurry up and pack just a few of your things. [*He smiles but his eyes are restless.*] Why have they believed me so quickly without subjecting me to close investigation? [*He moves near the web again.*]

[*Enter* CHRISTIE, *addressing someone off stage.*]

CHRISTIE: Yes, indeed, this is the house of Mr G. K. Ananse. Oh, taxi drivers! What comes out of their mouths sometimes is most amusing. He is calling me Mrs Ananse. [*Quite swollen-headed*] Mrs Ananse, eh? It does sound good. [*She is not aware that* ANANSE *is watching her. She calls out to the driver:*] My in-laws are coming right away, be patient.

[*Turning, she notices* ANANSE, *and is startled.*]

Oh, I didn't notice you in the corner there.

ANANSE: [*Moving towards her*] I know you didn't notice.

CHRISTIE: Really, what comes out of the mouths of taxi drivers sometimes is most amusing.

ANANSE: You have heard things you want to hear, haven't you?

MBOGUO

[PLAYERS *start the song 'I'm Down in a Pit'.* ANANSE, AYA,

ANANSE AND STORY-
TELLER IN THE
MBOGUO: Who is
knocking?

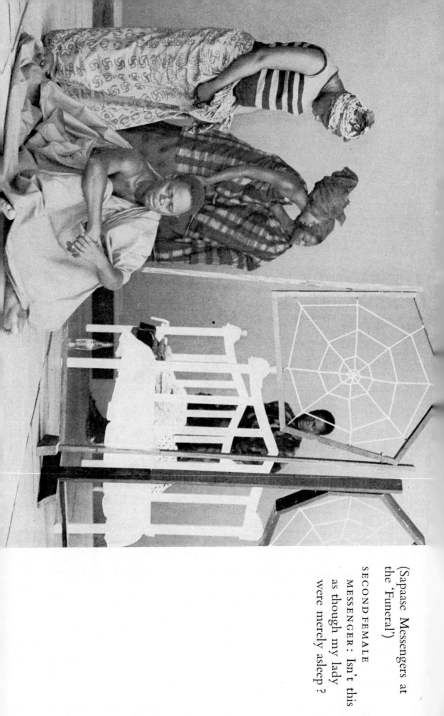

(Sapaase Messengers at the 'Funeral')

SECOND FEMALE
MESSENGER: Isn't this
as though my lady
were merely asleep?

EKUWA, CHRISTIE *and* PROPERTY MAN *mime a hurried carting out of luggage by chain service. Now and again it is clear that the song belongs to* AYA *and* EKUWA *and affects them most.*]

> I'm down in a pit
> And dying.
> I'm down in a pit
> And dying.
>
> Oh Yaa Baduwa!*
> I'm down in a pit
> And dying.
> I'm down in a pit
> And dying.
>
> I love work, love work,
> Work sickens now.
> Oh, go tell my mother
> I'm down in a pit
> And dying.
>
> Oh my clan.
>
> I'm down in a pit
> And dying.

[*The song ends with just* ANANSE *and* AYA *in transit.*]

AYA: [*On her way out now*] My grandchild Anansewa is enjoying such a deep sleep that I'm reluctant to wake her. When she wakes up, explain that my departure was an emergency. [*Hesitating*] Or shall I wake her? [ANANSE *catches her by the arm, diverting her.*]

EKUWA: [*In a great hurry on her way out*] Let's go, Aya, for the journey ahead of us is a long one.

ANANSE: That's true. What matters now is time. Investigate until you discover who it is that wants to ruin us.

AYA and EKUWA: You just wait!

ANANSE: I don't know if there's a possibility that my informant has exaggerated.

* Yaa Baduwa: name of the woman in distress in the song.

AYA: My son, once we arrive at Nanka, the truth will be revealed.

[ANANSE *follows them out.*]

STORYTELLER: I can't laugh enough. If this story of Ananse's were ending just here, I would laugh until my ribs protested. I wish I could have one eye looking on at Nanka as the taxi arrives with these two respectable ladies.

They will already be wailing while they are landing, or if they have chosen to be furious instead, they will be clamorous with insults. How bewildered Nanka citizens will be! I tell you, that if this were the end of the story, I wouldn't stop laughing.

But, friends, the branches of this story of the Marriage of Anansewa have multiplied. Here comes one of them.

[*Enter* CHRISTIE *walking pensively in from outside. Her eyes are staring at* STORYTELLER, *though she is not addressing him. He stands aside to watch her.*]

CHRISTIE: Whatever is George doing? Why doesn't he explain it to me?
STORYTELLER: Sister, don't ask me, he is your George.
CHRISTIE: It wasn't to you I was talking, brother. I was thinking, and my thoughts escaped. [*To herself again*] However, when I talked with him a little while ago, he did smile on me. Can it be that he sees I'm toiling for him? [*She sings:*]

> Can he see?
> Can he see
> That I love him
> And toiling for him
> Till I weary?
> Georgie!
> That he may smile on me.

[ANANSE, *entering unexpectedly, watches her unseen. On the next round, he sings with her and dances with her showing that what he hears pleases him.* CHRISTIE *is thrilled.*]

ANANSE: It is possible that I do see you are toiling for me. I can believe you are the one, more than anyone else I know in this world, who can assist me to do a deed of mine, which I'm forced to do in this house. Christie.

CHRISTIE: [*Lovingly*] Georgie. Speak.

ANANSE: From this evening through all day tomorrow until sunset the next day, we have something to do here which, to tell the truth, I couldn't call easy without lying.

CHRISTIE: Command me!

ANANSE: [*Taking her hand*] Very well, let's go and wake up Anansewa.

[CHRISTIE *starts her song again. They dance off. The* PLAYERS *now move out to the song 'Yaw Barima'* which ironically says Ayekoo!† to* ANANSE, *as would be said to a person who is hard at some honest work or trying to cope with a tough experience.*]

> Yaw Barima
> Ayekoo!
> Yaw Barima
> Ayekoo!
>
> Yaw Barima,
> I was beaten by the rain.
> Yaw Barima,
> Its after-drippings
> Made father die.
>
> Yaw Barima
> Ayekoo!
>
> E, e
> Yaw Barima,
> I was beaten by the rain.
> Yaw Barima,

* Yaw Barima: name of the man who has managed to endure the tragic experience in the song; the name Barima connotes a man of bravery.

† Ayekoo!: a standard expression of congratulation, addressed to someone working hard, or who has achieved something by hard labour.

Its after-drippings
Made father die.

Yaw Barima
Ayekoo!

END OF ACT THREE

Act Four

[*The* PLAYERS *have reassembled below the stage. Two* WOMEN *rush on to the stage with a half-dirging, half-weeping act. It is difficult to determine if they are pretending or serious*].

FIRST WOMAN: How could it happen?
                   They called in Dispenser* Hammond.
SECOND WOMAN: How could this thing happen?
                   They called in Dispenser Hammond.
TOGETHER: Oh, Dispenser Hammond!
                   Oh, oh!
                   They called in Dispenser Hammond.
                   Mhmm-m-m.

[*They tear off with 'Mhmm-m-m'.*]

STORYTELLER: [*Down where the players are, watching them disappear*]
Do you see what has happened in this neighbourhood? Parents are suffering in their guts for nothing. Oh, George K. Ananse.

[*The* TWO WOMEN *rush in again.*]

FIRST WOMAN: Oh, how could it happen?
                   They called in Dispenser Hammond.
SECOND WOMAN: How could this thing happen?
                   They called in Dispenser Hammond.
TOGETHER: Oh, Dispenser Hammond!
                   Oh, oh!
                   They called in Dispenser Hammond
                   Mhmm-m-m.

* Dispenser: pharmacist, but in its popular use practically meaning Doctor.

[*They tear off in a different direction.*]

STORYTELLER: I can't laugh enough. Listen, Ananse is lying, he is really, and so relax.

As for some people! They do not pause to enquire how true a thing is before they believe it, and so it's easy to deceive them.

You were here, weren't you, when Ananse started drilling his daughter, Anansewa, in pretending dead? Very well. It turns out that he did his work well.

And so, since Anansegoro doesn't take long to grow, time having passed, let me remind you that this is the day set by one of the four chiefs for his performance of the head-drink ceremony for Anansewa.

[*The* WOMEN *rush in again.*]

FIRST WOMAN: And so, how could this thing happen?
                 They called in Dispenser Hammond.
SECOND WOMAN: How could it happen?
                 They called in Dispenser Hammond.
TOGETHER: Oh, Dispenser Hammond!
                 Oh, oh!
                 They called in Dispenser Hammond.
                 Mhmm-m-m.

[*They pass through.* STORYTELLER *mounts the stage.*]

STORYTELLER: You'd better stop; better stop because they say the minute wailing sounds in Mr Ananse's ear, he wants to kill himself.

[*Addressing the audience:*]

Last night, everybody was asleep by the time the Methodist Church clock struck twelve o'clock.

[PROPERTY MAN *strikes this hour while* STORYTELLER *counts, leaping numbers to reach twelve o'clock quickly.*]

The town deserted, with nobody coming or going, suddenly there was Mr George K. Ananse's voice, screaming.

VOICE OF ANANSE: Come, somebody! Come to my aid! Ah, my one and only possession! I'm about to see disaster!

STORYTELLER: You hear that?

VOICE OF ANANSE: Alas! Anansewa! She has fainted! Something has descended on her! Where is everybody? Alas! Help! Help! People! People!

STORYTELLER: By the time people who heard this call arrived on the scene, there was Anansewa, lying as though she were dead. And then, you should have seen Ananse here.

VOICE OF ANANSE: Where are the doctors? Oh! Dispenser Hammond! Call in Dispenser Hammond! Ah! Ah! Ah!

STORYTELLER: Thereupon, one tears off this way, another that way. And as for Mr Ananse, he was by this time rolling on the ground, and striking his head violently against the wall, pum, pum, pum.

[PROPERTY MAN *produces the 'pum, pum' sound to help* STORYTELLER.]

Believe me, had there not been tough-muscled men present to restrain him, he would have done violence to himself and died instead.

Friends, Anansegoro doesn't take long to grow! There they were, trying, when suddenly Ananse springs up to stand at the door of the room in which his daughter lies, and invoking an oath, forbids anyone to touch his daughter. He declares, that having been afflicted by a catastrophe of this dimension, he will do violence to himself should anyone come close to him.

So that's how it has happened, that those who choose to believe it, believe that Anansewa is dead.

But, as for a funeral of this nature, a funeral for the Dead-and-Alive we will watch how it will be conducted this day.

[*He takes castanets out of his pocket and accompanies himself in a song.*]

Oh, Dead-and-Alive,
Oh, Dead-and-Alive,

> Anansewa e,
> You're due for the grave.
> Oh, Dead-and-Alive,
> How d'you get there?
>
> Is she dead?
> Is she dead?
> Is she dead?

[*Enter* CHRISTIE *from outside. She is in mourning, and is carrying a clan staff.*★ *She answers as though the* STORYTELLER *were asking her the question.*]

CHRISTIE: Oh, yes, sir. It is indeed hard to believe it.

STORYTELLER: [*Pretending commiseration*] Sorry. Isn't it a bitter story? How is a guest like you going to handle your responsibility for giving the news?

CHRISTIE: Ah, sir. [*She acts as though she is on the point of breaking into tears, and starts singing:*]

> How do I explain today?
> How do I explain today?
> How do I?
>
> Alas! None of his clan.
>
> How do I explain today?
> How do I?
>
> Alas! None of his clan.
>
> How do I explain today?
> How do I?

[*Speaking:*] I'm completely unable to suppress my sorrow, sir. And there's Pa Ananse, fainting at the mere sound of wailing.

> Alas! None of his clan.
>
> How do I explain today?
> How do I?

★ clan staff: a staff mounted by the identifying totemic symbol of a clan: in this case it is the staff of the Nsona clan whose totemic symbol is the crow.

[*She passes through, singing.*]
[*Playing his castanets* STORYTELLER *makes his statement in speech and song, the* PLAYERS *helping him in the song parts. He roams, proclaiming to the public:*]

STORYTELLER: Oh, I've thought, but I don't understand.
Do you understand?

Let's think it over and see.
Let's think it over and see
If we by any chance
Will be able to understand
The plan in Ananse's head,
Which has pressed his daughter so
To pretend to be dead
Because of the knotty fix
Entangling her father
And giving him a headache.

[*Singing:*] Oh, Dead-and-Alive,
Oh, Dead-and-Alive,

Anansewa e,
You're due for the grave.
Oh, Dead-and-Alive,
How do you get there?

[*Speaking:*] Let me say what I think, then.
No-sale-no-payment
Obliges no one.

The point about head-drink is
That it's paid for the living.
Therefore, Chief-of-Sapaase e!
Don't bother to come,
Oh, don't bother to come,
Because the object of your interest
Did not survive for you,
Did not survive for you.

[*Singing:*] Oh, Dead-and-Alive,
Oh, Dead-and-Alive,

63

Anansewa,
You're due for the grave.
Oh, Dead-and-Alive
How d'you get there?

[*Speaking:*] Oh-h-h-h, Chief-of-the-Mines,
The point about head-drink is
That it's paid for the living.

And there is Chief, not knowing
That the case seems to be—

[*Singing:*] Oh, Dead-and-Alive,
Oh, Dead-and-Alive,
Anansewa,
You're due for the grave.

Oh, Dead-and-Alive,
How d'you get there?

[*Speaking:*] Oh-h-h-h, Togbe Klu!
Don't bother to come,
Oh, don't bother to come,
Because the object of your interest
Did not survive for you.

And Chief, he happens to be
Far, far, far away,
He doesn't know it's a case of—

[*Singing:*] Oh, Dead-and-Alive
Oh, Dead-and-Alive
Anansewa,
You're due for the grave.

Oh, Dead-and-Alive
How d'you get there?

[*Speaking:*] Oh, Chief-Who-Is-Chief,
Oh, she didn't survive.
As for you, Chief,
You were most highly expected,
And yet, the turn of events

Has made it essential
That you also should be treated
Along with the rest on the basis
Of no-sale-no-payment.

As for you, Chief, were I to get you
In private somewhere
I would give you the hint that it's—

[*Singing:*] Oh, Dead-and-Alive,
Oh, Dead-and-Alive,
Anansewa,
You're due for the grave.

Oh, Dead-and-Alive,
How d'you get there?

Is she dead?
Is she dead?
Is she dead?

[STORYTELLER *has come down among the audience, with whom he
continues to think the matter over.*]

STORYTELLER: What do you think? All of us have seen this knot
that has been tied. How do you suppose Mr Ananse will untie
it? As far as the four chiefs' problem is concerned, since nobody
marries a corpse that part of the knot can be considered untied.
Moreover, there isn't any law to oblige Ananse to return to
them any of the gifts he has received from their hands so far
and used to improve his circumstances.

But I ask you, this Dead-and-Alive with whom he is closeted
in there, and whom it is impossible to take to the grave; how
can he so hide her that nothing of his deceit shall be exposed?
What would you do, if you were Ananse?

Should he cause her to vanish?

To Ouagadougou?
To Mexico?
To Kenya?
Or India?

Or is it that
Anansewa herself
Will now turn to

[*Singing:*]   Wind, wind, wind? [*Echo from Anansewa's song.*]

[*Laughing,* STORYTELLER *sits down with the audience. The* PLAYERS *start the song* 'I'm Down in a Pit' *again, singing it solemnly.* PROPERTY MAN *walks sneakingly in to set two web screens.*]

STORYTELLER: [*Rising and making his way to join the* PLAYERS] That's the nature of Anansegoro. Anansegoro is such that as soon as you release your mind to it it takes you, penetrating where it might not have been possible for you to go. Do you notice that since we started thinking, we also have arrived right where the eye of the story is?

[*The* PLAYERS *increase the volume of their singing.* ANANSE *and* CHRISTIE *sneak in carrying a bed which they set behind the web screens. They communicate in whispers, their movements are speedy. As soon as the bed is in place,* PROPERTY MAN, *in mourning, enters carrying a chair, and is directed by* ANANSE *to sit at the entrance.* CHRISTIE *fetches the clan staff which* ANANSE *gives to* PROPERTY MAN *to hold. Producing a sheet of paper and a pencil from her clothes,* CHRISTIE *reads it and speaks like one suppressing tears.*]

CHRISTIE: I have called Akate and informed Togbe Klu, and they are on their way.

ANANSE: Let your voice quiver a little more so that you'll be in practice.

CHRISTIE: I have called Sapaase Palace and informed them. They say they are on their way.

I have called the Mines and informed them. They may even have arrived already. [*Her voice is now quivering as much as possible.*] I have called Chief-Who-Is-Chief and informed him. [*She sobs.*] Hmmm.

[*The volume of the singing increases and one of the* WOMEN *recites* 'How could it happen' *intermittently in a subdued voice. With great stealth* ANANSE *walks round the bed. The song ceases. He takes a large watch out of his pocket and reads it.*]

ANANSE: The time is up. My soul, Kweku, support me, for I'm weary. Life is really a struggle. Should this moment in which I'm trapped by any chance miscarry, I'm finished. And if care is not taken, I will, moreover, strike the fortune from my daughter's lips and spill it completely. Man is pathetic.

As I stand here, the fear attacking me is overwhelming; still I will take it this way, that I have seized hold of the tail of a wild beast who will bite me if I let go. So I'm holding on to it. What else can I do?

I know that not all my ways can be considered straight. But, before God, I'm not motivated by bad thoughts at this moment. I have a deep fatherly concern for this only child of mine. If the world were not what it is, I would not gamble with such a priceless possession. So what I plead is this: may grace be granted so that from among the four chiefs who desire to marry my child, the one will reveal himself who will love her and take good care of her when I give her to him.

[*He walks slowly to call* ANANSEWA *from the next room. He is indeed weary.*]

Anansewa—a! Come, the time is up.

[*The* PLAYERS *continue singing 'I'm Down in a Pit' solemnly.* ANANSEWA *runs in, and throws herself on the bed.* ANANSE *and* CHRISTIE *speedily arrange her. A voice outside calls out 'Agoo!' for permission to enter.* CHRISTIE *dashes out.* ANANSE *rushes outside the web screens on tiptoe, and sits on the floor as miserably as possible.* PROPERTY MAN *organises himself. The song ceases as* CHRISTIE *leads in the* MINES MESSENGERS. *They are two men.*]

CHRISTIE: [*As she enters*] Is the elder of the family there? Here are messengers from the Mines.

[ANANSE *groans, and lurches sideways as though he is fainting.* CHRISTIE *dashes across to support him.*]

Pa George! Suppress the agony a little. I have explained what agonising scenes you cannot face. It's because there are customary routines to follow that they feel obliged to come. Respectable messengers, you have permission.

[*She gestures in the direction of the bed, and leads them round it.*]

FIRST MESSENGER: Look, she seems as though she is merely asleep.
CHRISTIE: You see! Anansewa is deceiving us so much. As you look at her, it seems as though she is about to rise any minute. And yet, we know that it's we who are vainly indulging in sweet anticipation.

[ANANSE *groans.*]

Please, Pa George, suppress it a little.

[*She indicates where the* MESSENGERS *should stand.* PROPERTY MAN *moves over to stand by her.*]

FIRST MESSENGER: Respected lady, and you, elder of the family, whom we meet here. We do not like the reason for our coming here, but we are obliged to come. We were in no way expecting that on this day we would come on such a journey. Our royal one, the wealthy paramount Chief of the Mines whose praise-name is 'You Are Coming Again, Aren't You', has had many discussions with his councillors about this marriage he was going to contract. He insisted—against their advice—that if a lady of this quality came into his hands she would give enlightened training to the many children to whom his wives have given birth.

[ANANSE *groans.*]

It has not been our royal one's fortune to hear the news he was expecting. He who is Owner has snatched his property from our royal one's hands.

[ANANSE *groans hard.*]

We will be brief, sir, Our royal one has this to say: that because this lady had not yet become his wife, he cannot give her burial; but that which custom does permit, he is not reluctant to fulfil.

[PROPERTY MAN *carries in the required props. At the mention of each item he hands it over.*]

He sends this bolt of silk; this kente from Bonwire; this dumas cotton cloth. Use them for dressing his lady's bed for her.

He sends this drink, and this bag of money to help her father pay for the funeral in farewell to his lady.

[*The other messenger, receiving the articles one by one from* PROPERTY MAN, *hands them over to* CHRISTIE. *Having received them all she shows them to* ANANSE, *then she enters the screened-off area, places the cloths on the bed, and the drink beside it. Returning, she confers in whispers with* ANANSE, *her mouth close to his ear.*]

CHRISTIE: Respected messengers, Pa Ananse says he has heard the message you bring.

[ANANSE *keels over.* CHRISTIE *quickly holds him up, patting him to comfort him. She breaks into song, and gesturing the* MESSENGERS *to follow her, leads them out.*]

CHRISTIE: Oh really clueless one
                   Wailing though I lack skill
                   Oh really clueless one.
ANANSE: [*Rising*] Ah! So had my daughter gone into this marriage, this chief's councillors would not have liked it; and she would have gone there to get hated. Very well, I have untied that part of the knot.

[*He and* PROPERTY MAN *sneak in to see if all is well with the bed. They hear* CHRISTIE'S *voice calling 'Agoo! Agoo!' urgently and dash back to their positions.* CHRISTIE *leads in* SAPAASE MESSENGERS, *two women and a man.*]

CHRISTIE: [*To* PROPERTY MAN] Is the elder of the family there? Here come messengers from Sapaase Palace.

[ANANSE *groans.*]

Pa George! [*She goes over to support him.*] My mothers, this is what I told you about. He is taking it extremely hard.

MALE MESSENGER: Pa Ananse, condolences. We will make it brief. What has to be done must be done, and that is why we came. We are not here to do any agonising things to bruise your pain.

FIRST FEMALE MESSENGER: Oh, where is my lady? Listen, I'll carry you on my back. Place my lady on my back so that I can take her to my chief. Our royal one, you have our sympathy. Pa George, condolences; d'you hear?

[ANANSE *groans.*]

CHRISTIE: Mama, mama, mama. Stop it, stop it, stop it.

[*She starts her song 'Oh Really Clueless One', gestures in the direction of the bed and leads the* MESSENGERS *to walk round it.*]

SECOND FEMALE MESSENGER: Isn't this as though my lady were merely asleep? Ah, Pa Ananse, my sympathy. Our royal one, sympathy is yours also. My lady, you are lovely. I was campaigning for you so that I could get a beautiful baby from your womb to carry on my back, and display my pride for the purpose of putting to shame a certain bitchy, ugly, somebody who is there in Sapaase Palace.

ANANSE: Stop it. Stop it.

MALE MESSENGER: Very well, sir.

FIRST FEMALE MESSENGER: Alas! My lady, I was anxious for you to come into residence in the top storey of the palace, and then, we would have sent packing downstairs—straight!—that shrew of a woman at large there, who is only waiting to claw out our eyes and scare us away.

[ANANSE *groans.*]

MALE MESSENGER: Enough, mother. [CHRISTIE *points out where they should stand.*] Well, elders of the house whom we meet here, we will be brief. Who likes bitterness? Were we not obliged to come, this journey would have been too bitter and too hard to face. Having come, we are well aware that it is the father who is most afflicted; therefore if you ask us not to do agonising things in his presence, we agree with you.

Had our royal one acquired this lady, a certain nasty beast, who is at large in his home, would have fled on her own accord, and peace would have come to the home.

Truly, we are hurt, because we were paying conscientious attention, as you know. It was as though we were regularly bringing our eggs into storage here, accumulating them for collection later. And the time was just rounding the corner too; but The Implacable One said no. Our eggs have hatched nothingness, leaving us with empty hands.

[ANANSE *groans.*]

I've cut it short, sir. When our royal one discussed the news with his council, some were of the opinion that since this is a case of no-sale-no-payment other families would simply consider the matter concluded. But our particular family is endowed with such compassion that we ourselves would not consider it nice if we did nothing for you. Therefore, what our royal one has to say is this: he has no right to give burial to this child because the head-drink did not come in time to make it a conclusive marriage. You yourselves are well aware that had our royal one not been thoroughly knowledgeable about customary procedure, he would not be occupying his ancient stool. He says that he is not reluctant at all to perform whatever custom he has the right to perform in farewell to the woman he loves.

[*As he names the things they have brought, one woman receives them item by item from* PROPERTY MAN *and passes them on to* CHRISTIE.]

Here are his silk, his velvet, his white kente cloth, his white striped cloth; place them on his beloved's bed for her to take to the grave. Here is his cash donation of twenty guineas also; spend it on drinks for the funeral. That's the mission that brought us here.

[CHRISTIE *shows* ANANSE *these things and places them on the bed. Returning, she consults him in whispers before she speaks.*]

CHRISTIE: He says he has received your message in full.

[*After a brief hesitation she leads the* MESSENGERS *out, sorrowfully singing her song again.*]

ANANSE: Such verbal agility and trouble-ridden talk.

> The world is dark
> Is dark
> The world is really dark.

[*He rises.*] Had you people got hold of my child, you would have involved her, blameless as she is, in your contention in Sapaase Palace and driven that wild woman of whom you speak to kill her and bereave me for nothing.

It is the Lord I thank, for I would have pushed my child into disaster. All right, I have untied that part of the knot also.

[*He and* PROPERTY MAN *enter the screened area. Almost immediately they hear the clanging of a gong, followed by singing. They fly back to their positions. With 'Agoo! Agoo!'* CHRISTIE *leads in* AKATE MESSENGERS, *two men.*]

AKATE MESSENGERS: Zoxome mele du yom lo!
>> Togbi Klu be, 'Zixome mele du yom'
>> Kaka made kasia, Ku do aba di
>>> na Anansewa!
>> Amega 'megawo va so di koto,
>>> ne woa tsoe adi.
>> Ao! Anansewa tso da yibo tso
>>> yi Avli mee!

CHRISTIE: [*She waits for the song to end.*] Elder of the family, you have heard with your own ears. Togbe Klu's messengers have arrived.

[*She indicates a place outside the screens where they move to view* ANANSEWA *through the web. They shake their heads in sorrow and sing again movingly.* ANANSE *groans.*]

CHRISTIE: George, please control yourself so that they can deliver their news.

FIRST MESSENGER: Togbe Ananse and his elders whom we meet here, we come as direct brothers of Togbe Klu IV. In all Akate we are the ones who know what preparations our brother and our chief has endeavoured to make as he awaits Togbe Ananse's child. Our brother was most appreciative of this lady's training in secretarial work. He was looking forward to having a real helper at last to assist him in building up a substantial business. A helper who would not ruin him as some of his own relatives, I regret to say, have done time and time again to his distress. Look, he is ready to order giant trucks for bringing cattle from Mali. That aside, he has ordered a trawler, for fishing. And the documents for all these were to have been entrusted to his own wife's administration.

[ANANSE *groans.*]

Had this misfortune occurred in the days when Togbe's spirit would quicken at the recital of his praise-name, 'Prickly-Pear', Akate town would be in a turmoil that would overflow to this place also. This funeral house wouldn't be so silent.

But these days, he has become a most zealous adherent of a Spiritualist Church, and so when something happens which he cannot fathom he leaves it in God's hands no matter how much he is pained. When he heard the news he wept so much we also wept. But he has left it in God's hands in the same way. He was not even in favour of our coming here. What was the use, he said. But we said, 'No'. We have not yet had the vision he has had, which leads him to that point of view. Even if we came to do nothing, we would show our faces here. Togbe Ananse, condolences.

[ANANSE *bows his head;* CHRISTIE *moves over to consult him in whispers.*]

CHRISTIE: He says I should ask you if that is all you have to say.
FIRST MESSENGER: That is all.
CHRISTIE: He says he thanks you for your affection.
MESSENGERS: [*Together*] Boba no lo
                 Ha we ga kpe lo

[*They sing their song to the gong as they depart, led by* CHRISTIE. ANANSE *sits staring into the distance; he shakes his head regretfully.*]

ANANSE: Ah! Togbe Klu. You whom I even forgot sometimes to count among those in the race, lo and behold, it is you who turns out to be the one with such good intentions. You should have given me that understanding, for I had no idea it was your desire to live so well with my child. [*He thinks.*]

    Have I allowed your messengers to depart? What if Chief-Who-Is-Chief doesn't come? And if he does, supposing he comes in the manner in which the Mines people and Sapaase people came? What would I do then? If in desperation and torment, I push my child into his hands in that event, I would be pushing her into catastrophe. Oh, has trouble so turned into a fallen tree across my road? Is there no rest at all in this life? Hmm, my mind is exhausted.

[*He moves beside* ANANSEWA. CHRISTIE *shouts 'Agoo!'* ANANSE *darts into hiding behind the web screens.* PROPERTY MAN *rearranges himself.* CHRISTIE *leads in* MESSENGERS OF CHIEF-WHO-IS-CHIEF.]

CHRISTIE: Pa George? [*She doesn't see him.*] Has Pa George gone? [*She sees him.*] Pa George. [*Her voice quivers.*] Your loving ones want you. Indeed, today, I really can't escape dealing with an issue too weighty for my competence.

[ANANSE *leaves the web, and walks out to slump down in his place.*]

My honourable ones, see how miserably he sits. It's he, the

father; we are finding it more unbearable to look at him. Had there not been tough-muscled men around to help, we would have buried him instead by now; you would not have met him here alive. A little more delay and you would not have been here in time to view the face of this beloved one of yours either.

ANANSE: Honourable messengers of the great one, have you arrived? I am worth nothing in your sight indeed. I promised you that I would take good care of that precious possession of yours entrusted to me. But I failed to prime my gun and stand firm to defend her.

What shall I say to you? Shall I merely say 'Sorry' to you?

[*The* MESSENGERS *whip out their handkerchiefs in unison, and dab their eyes.*]

CHRISTIE: Pa George, don't. My honourable ones, it was for you we were waiting. Because of what the father is doing, we were going to bury the child out of his sight, according to his instructions. Come, then, and view what is yours.

[*She leads them round the bed, wailing in song.*]

> Wailing for my child,
> Anansewa, don't blame me.
> Wailing for my child,
> Anansewa, don't blame me.
> Wailing,
> One, alone, Anansewa.
>
> Don't blame me,
> Wailing,
> Without skill but wailing,
> Anansewa.

[*At the end of the song she points out where the* MESSENGERS *should stand.*]

FIRST MESSENGER: Lady, and elders whom we meet here, forgive us for delaying a little, but the orders which our chief who is so

75

unexpectedly afflicted gave us, enjoined that we should not come on this mission inadequately prepared. Therefore, we were making every effort to assemble everything before setting out. The fires are so totally out, where we come from.

All the way here, we've been painfully regretful. We have this much to say, that if we had been aware that Chief-Who-Is-Chief loved the lady Anansewa with a love so deep we would have seen to settling her by his side without any delay. Had she come to him this might probably not have happened. The time was just rounding the corner too. He has called a meeting of very important people at the palace a week from this very day to fix the day of the wedding and plan all the arrangements before sending word to the lady's father.

What more shall I say to make everyone understand the pathetic plight of our royal one, Chief-Who-Is-Chief?

[ANANSE *keels over and springs up in such agony that* PROPERTY MAN *goes to his aid.*]

CHRISTIE: Sirs, that's what I told you.

FIRST MESSENGER: I will stop there and deliver the message we bring. There is a man who is hailed by the praise-name Fire-Extinguisher. He is Chief-Who-Is-Chief and he has sent us to the respected Mr George K. Ananse.

He says that he makes no error in calling this man his father-in-law, because had Ungenerous Death not snatched this child from his hands, it would be in order so to address him.

This Chief-Who-Is-Chief, who was eager to blend his blood with yours and become a member of your family, wishes me to inform you about his painful grief, and add that he accepts total responsibility for everything concerning the woman who had but one more step to take to enter his home.

Therefore, from his hands to yours here are all requirements for her funeral.

[PROPERTY MAN *brings in the things which one of the women receives from him item by item and hands over to* CHRISTIE.]

Here is the ring a husband places on a wife's finger. Here is a bag of money, spend it on the funeral. Here are cloths which any woman who is confidently feminine would select with a careful eye; place them on his beloved one's bed; dumas, white kente, silk kente, velvet, brocade.

The drinks he sends to help his father-in-law with the funeral are in such quantities that we couldn't bring them in here. We needn't even pay attention to that because this . . . [*He himself receives a bottle from* PROPERTY MAN] . . . this bottle of Schnapps in my hand is what it is absolutely mandatory for me to place in your hands. His wishes are that this must be the drink with which the farewell libation is poured when his beloved one is being placed in the coffin.

[ANANSE *groans.*]

Finally, it is his desire to do for Anansewa what a husband does for a wife. And so he sends his coffin, one made of glass. Place his wife in it for him. [*A momentary hush.*] Lady, bring your elders along, so that I can show you the coffin.

[*The* MESSENGERS *lead* CHRISTIE *and* PROPERTY MAN *to the entrance from where the viewing takes place. Overcome by grief, they whip out their handkerchiefs at the same time and dab their eyes.* ANANSE *springs up, moves over to take a look for himself and wails.*]

ANANSE: Is this my adversity? What have I done that I'm stripped to such nakedness? My child, such was your fortune, and you are so silent? Ah, life does wield a whip that the human being cannot withstand.

[*He falls back into somebody's arms.*]

Ah, sirs, this place has become awesome.

[*It is as though he is going into a trance.*]

Give me drink to pour libation myself.
Give me the drink my child's lover has sent.

[CHRISTIE *hands over the drink to* PROPERTY MAN *who passes it on to* ANANSE. *He is given a glass into which he pours a portion. He moves into the screened-off area, leans against the web and starts the libation.*]

> Dependable God,
> I'm calling on you,
> Earth Efuwa;
> Souls who have preceded us,
> Come, all of you,
> Here is your drink.
> What we receive
> We share with you.
>
> If you have gone, it does not mean
> You have neglected us.
> You are with us
> In difficulty and in joy.
>
> I am announcing to you
> That your grandchild is on her way.
> Condolences to you,
> Condolences to us.
>
> We know you are there
> To give her a welcome embrace.
> We know it is to her family she comes,
> And that being so,
> We should be comforted.
> But there is more to it than that,
> Ancestors, there is more to it than that.

[*He goes into a trance.*]

> You who are lying there!
> Anansewa!
> I'm calling you!
> Listen with the ancestors;
>
> Chief-Who-Is-Chief
> The-man-fit-for-a-husband
> Has sent his money

[CHRISTIE *places it on the bed.*]

Has sent his cloths

[CHRISTIE *places them on the bed.*]

Has sent his drink
Which I hold in my hand;

A person who is so wise,
A person who so understands what love is
That though the feast has not yet been spread
For him to feed,
He has sent his thanks;

See, there stands his coffin
Giving proof of his love,
Giving proof
That for Anansewa's sake
He is doing far more than
What custom prescribes for him;
Anansewa had yet to enter this man's home
Yet, see how he has done
What a real husband does, in full.

[*He goes into an even deeper trance.*]

Ancestors, I am pleading with you,
If it is your desire
As it is ours
That Chief-Who-Is-Chief
Should marry Anansewa,
See to it that she returns to life!

Wake her!
See to it that Anansewa awakes
And returns to become a bride!

[*He falls into the arms of* PROPERTY MAN *as though he is overcome by contact with the spirits. He sings like a man in a trance.*]

> Wake, oh wake
> Oh wake, oh wake.
>
> Kweku's child, Anansewa,
> Wake, oh wake!
>
> Love is calling you, return,
> Wake, oh wake!
>
> Chief-Who-Is-Chief loves you true
> Wake, oh wake!

[*He moves swiftly to* ANANSEWA's *side and walks round the bed staring at her. There is a hush.*]

ANANSE: [*Suddenly*] Oh, she is waking. Are there such wonders in the world? My child is waking.

[ANANSEWA *stirs.*]

Does love have such power? Christie, open the doors and let everybody in to see the power of amazing love.

[CHRISTIE *and* PROPERTY MAN *mime opening up the house, and beckon people in. The* PLAYERS *surge all over the place.*]

There is my child, awakened for me by love. How strong love is. Love has awakened my child.

> She is rising!
> She is rising!
> She has risen, complete.

[ANANSEWA *springs out of the bed, causing* MESSENGERS *and all the others to scatter and hover round in bewilderment. But* ANANSE, CHRISTIE *and* PROPERTY MAN *huddle around* ANANSEWA *hugging one another, and shaking hands.*]

ANANSEWA: [*Just like one suddenly woken from a deep sleep*] Father! Where is father? Father.
ANANSE: My lovely child. My one and only daughter. Here I am.

[ANANSEWA *smiles and nestles her head in his bosom.*]

ANANSEWA: Father, I could hear Chief-Who-Is-Chief calling me.
ANANSE: He was indeed calling you. His love has won a victory for us all. [*The guests express much amazement.*] Honourable messengers, I'm dumbfounded. Here, alive, is your precious possession. It is by the grace of the God who never gives us up. I believe that there is nothing better for you to do now than to return to break the news of this miracle to my loving son-in-law, so that his bitterness shall turn to sweetness. Thank you for coming on such a consoling journey.

Friends who brought your compassion in to cover my nakedness in my grief, I thank you. By the day of my birth, if our spirits which fled from us return to us, and I don't invite you all to meet here for a great celebration, may no parent call me George Kweku Ananse.

Christie!
CHRISTIE: Georgie!
ANANSE: Rare helper! Supporter, your thanks await you.

[*He hugs* CHRISTIE *and* ANANSEWA.]

STORYTELLER: [*Bursting into laughter and crying out*] That's Kweku all right!
ANANSE: [*Starting*] Goodness! Look, sir, leave the praise-singing alone till some other time, and instead, manage the guests' departure for me, to end this whole event right now.
STORYTELLER: [*Still laughing*] I understand you too well. In that case, friends, we will end this Anansegoro right here. Whether you found it interesting or not, do take parts of it away, leaving parts of it with me. We are shaking hands for departure.

[*The* PLAYERS *sing joyfully, shaking hands with* ANANSEWA, CHRISTIE *and* PROPERTY MAN.]

Oh, oh,

Is love's power so strong?
Is love's power so strong?

So strong?
Is love's power so strong?

Let's relate in love
That we may thrive—

True love is rare.

Let's relate in love
That we may thrive—

True giver is rare.

Let's relate in love
That we may thrive—

True helper is rare.

Let's relate in love
That we may thrive—

Thank you, chief so rare.

Let's relate in love
That we may thrive—

Thank you, husband rare.

Let's relate in love
That we may thrive.

CURTAIN

African Creative Writing Series

The African Creative Writing Series, under the general editorship of Professor Michael J. C. Echeruo, is being launched to give readers the very best in African plays, poetry and novels.
The first three titles to be published in the series are:

EFUA T. SUTHERLAND *The Marriage of Anansewa*, a comedy about the naive and rascally attempts of Ananse to make money by betrothing his daughter to several rich chiefs simultaneously.
ISBN 0 582 64139 X

UMARU LADAN and DEXTER LYNDERSAY *Shaihu Umar*, a play based on the novel by Sir Abubakar Tafawa Balewa. The Hausa hero relates the dramatic and moving story of his life while the events he describes are taking place on stage. ISBN 0 582 64192 6

OMUNJAKKO NAKIBIMBIRI *The Sobbing Sounds*, the frank and revealing autobiography of an audacious young African with a lust for life. ISBN 0 582 64157 8

Creative Writing Already Published Includes

Novels and Short Stories:

GABRIEL RUHUMBIKA *Village in Uhuru*
A novel about the far-reaching effects of *uhuru*—independence upon the people of a remote island village in Tanzania.

ISBN O 582 64011 3

CHRISTINA AMA ATA AIDOO *No Sweetness Here*
A collection of short stories in which the author explores a variety of themes with skill and understanding.

ISBN O 582 64037 7

PEGGY APPIAH *A Smell of Onions*
A collection of gently humorous vignettes of life in a typical Asante village.   ISBN O 582 64076 8

Plays:

EFUA T. SUTHERLAND *Edufa*
The conflict between traditional belief and modern circumstances forces a personal crisis upon Edufa, a successful young Ghanaian.

ISBN O 582 64029 6

CHRISTINA AMA ATA AIDOO *Anowa*
Rejecting the suitors her parents favour, Anowa insists on choosing her own husband, only to find herself facing insurmountable problems.   ISBN O 582 64031 8

CHRISTINA AMA ATA AIDOO *The Dilemma of a Ghost*
The tensions in the relationship between a Ghanaian and his Afro-American wife, who antagonises his family by her rejection of traditional customs.   ISBN O 582 60836 8

Poetry:

MICHAEL J. C. ECHERUO *Mortality*
A collection of poems by the distinguished Nigerian writer, scholar and critic.   ISBN 0 582 64033 4

JOHN PEPPER CLARK *A Reed in the Tide*
A selection of poems by one of Africa's most celebrated poets.
                                                ISBN 0 582 64007 5

JOHN PEPPER CLARK   *Casualties*
A record of the poet's reactions to the 'unspeakable events that all but tore apart Nigeria'.   ISBN 0 582 64058 X